BE RESTORED

Be Restored

WARREN W. WIERSBE

While this book is intended for the reader's personal enjoyment and profit, it is also designed for group study. Study questions are located at the end of the text.

Run So That You May Win
ivictor.com

Victor is an imprint of
Cook Communications Ministries, Colorado Springs, Colorado 80918
Cook Communications, Paris, Ontario
Kingsway Communications, Eastbourne, England

BE RESTORED
© 2002 by Warren W. Wiersbe

First Printing, 2002
Printed in the United States of America

2 3 4 5 6 7 8 9 10 Printing/Year 06 05 04 03 02

Editor: John Conaway, Craig Bubeck
Cover Design: iDesignEtc.

CONTENTS

PREFACE

Second Samuel begins with the death of Saul, Israel's first king, and ends with the death of David, Israel's greatest king. The book tells how God enabled David to unite the twelve tribes into one nation, defeat their enemies, expand their borders, and prepare the way for Solomon to ascend the throne. Parallel passages in 1 Chronicles supplement the "prophetic" account in 2 Samuel and give us the priestly point of view.

One of the major themes of 2 Samuel is *restoration*—the restoration of national unity, the restoration of David after he sinned, and the restoration of the throne after Absalom's rebellion. Intertwined with this theme is the emphasis on *power*, showing how God empowered David and his people to accomplish His will. Saul tore things apart, but God used David to start putting things back together again.

But alas, the events recorded here weren't always honoring to the Lord or beneficial to His people. Until the nation was united under David, political ambition and civil war led to the tragic deaths of too many people. As a consequence of David's sin with Bathsheba and his subsequent deception, David's own family was torn apart and the nation plunged into a second civil war. David didn't always have an easy time wearing the crown or wielding the sword, but the Lord was with His servant and ready to forgive when the king repented and confessed his sins. Then things began to heal up again.

If the life of David teaches us anything it's that God can use imperfect people to accomplish His purposes, though He lovingly disciplines when His servants disobey Him. David was a "man after God's own heart" (1 Sam. 13:14), but David was still a man and knew the weaknesses of human flesh. This book also teaches us that no personal or national situation is beyond the Lord's ability to put things right. David's legacy was a united people and a strong kingdom. He turned over to his son Solomon all he needed to do the one thing David wanted to do more than anything else—build a temple for the Lord.

We live in a shattered and fragmented world, but God's eternal goal is to bring all things together in Christ (Eph. 1:10). God is looking for men and women who will yield to His power and help restore broken lives, homes, churches, cities, and nations. Are you available?

Warren W. Wiersbe

A Suggested Outline of 2 Samuel

Key Theme: The restoration of the nation of Israel by God's power
Key Verse: 2 Samuel 22:29-31

    David unites the people. 1–7
    A new king. 1:1–5:5
    A new capital city. 5:6–6:23
    A new dynasty. 7:1-29

I. David expands the borders. 8:1–10:19
        He defeats Israel's enemies. 8:1-14; 10:1-19
        He organizes the kingdom. 8:15-18
        He honors Mephibosheth. 9:1-13

II. David disobeys the Lord. 11:1–20:26
        David's sins. 11:1–12:31
        Amnon's sins. 13:1-22
        Absalom's sins. 13:23–19:8
        David's return to Jerusalem. 19:9–20:26

III. David closes his reign. 21:1–24:25
        Showing respect for Saul. 21:1-14
        Defeating the Philistines. 21:15-22
        Praising the Lord. 22:1–23:7
        Honoring his mighty men. 23:8-38
        Buying a site for the temple. 24:1-15

A Suggested Outline of 1 Chronicles

Ancestry: genealogy of the twelve tribes. 1–9
Unity: the nation brought together. 10–16
Dynasty: God's covenant with David. 17
Victory: the borders expanded. 18–21
Efficiency: the nation organized. 22–29

I. The temple ministry. 22–26; 28:1–29:20
II. The army. 27
III. The heir to the throne. 28–29

ONE

2 SAMUEL 1:1–2:7
(SEE ALSO 1 CHRONICLES 10:1-12)

David, King of Judah

For ten years David was an exile with a price on his head, fleeing from Saul and waiting for the time when God would put him on the throne of Israel. During those difficult years, David grew in faith and godly character, and God equipped him for the work He had chosen him to do. When the day of victory did arrive, David was careful not to force himself on the people, many of whom were still loyal to the house of Saul. He took a cautious approach, and we can't help but admire David for his wisdom and patience as he won the affection and allegiance of the people and sought to unify the shattered nation. "So he shepherded them according to the integrity of his heart, and guided them by the skillfulness of his hands" (Ps. 78:72 NKJV).

1. Vindication (2 Sam. 1:1-16)
The Lord prevented David and his men from assisting the Philistines in their battle against Saul and Israel, so David returned to Ziklag. There he discovered that the Amalekites had invaded and taken all the people and goods and had left the town in ruins. God in His providence led David to the Amalekite camp. David routed the enemy, delivered the women and chil-

dren, and reclaimed all the goods as well as the loot the Amalekites had collected in their raids. He then returned to Ziklag and awaited a report from the battlefield (1 Sam. 29–30).

A *deceitful messenger (2 Sam. 1:1-10)*. On the day that David was slaughtering the Amalekites, the Philistines were overpowering Saul and his army at Mount Gilboa, where they killed Saul and three of his sons (1 Sam. 31; 1 Chron. 10:1-12). The next day, while David was returning to Ziklag, the Philistines were humiliating Saul by desecrating his body and the bodies of his sons, and the Amalekite messenger was starting off to bring the news to David. It took him at least three days to get to Ziklag, which was about eighty miles from the scene of the battle. So it was on David's third day in Ziklag that he received the tragic news that Israel had been defeated and that Saul and three of his sons were dead.[1]

Scripture gives us three accounts of the death of Saul and his sons: 1 Samuel 31:1-13, the report of the messenger in 2 Samuel 1:1-10, and the record in 1 Chronicles 10:1-14. According to 1 Chronicles 10:4-5, Saul killed himself by falling on his sword, but the messenger said he had killed Saul to save him from experiencing further agony and humiliation. 1 Chronicles 10:14 informs us that it was God who killed Saul for his rebellion, especially the sin of seeking guidance from a medium. Only with great difficulty can the reports in 1 Samuel 31 and 1 Chronicles 10 be reconciled with the report of the messenger; therefore, it's likely the man was lying.

There's no question that the man had been on the battlefield. While he was searching for spoils, he found the corpses of Saul and his sons before the Philistines had identified them, and he took Saul's insignias of kingship, his golden armband, and the gold chaplet he wore on his helmet. However, the Amalekite didn't kill Saul as he claimed, because Saul and his sons were already dead. But by claiming that he did, he lost his own life.[2]

One of the key words in this chapter is *fallen*, found in verses 4, 10, 12, 19, and 27. When Saul began his royal career, he was described as standing head and shoulders "taller than any of the people" (1 Sam. 9:2; see 1 Sam. 10:23 and 16:7), but he ended his career a fallen king. He fell on his face in fear in the house of the spirit medium (1 Sam. 28:20), and he fell on the battlefield before the enemy (1 Sam. 31:4). David humbled himself before the Lord, and the Lord lifted him up; but Saul's pride and rebellion brought him to a shameful end. "Therefore let him who thinks he stands take heed lest he fall" (1 Cor. 10:12 NKJV).[3] Saul was anointed king at the dawning of a new day (1 Sam. 9:26-27), but he chose to walk in the darkness (1 Sam. 28:8) and disobey the will of God.

A grieving camp (2 Sam. 1:11-12). The Amalekite messenger must have been shocked and then afraid when he saw David and his men tearing their garments and mourning the death of Saul. He thought that everybody in Ziklag would rejoice to hear the news of Saul's death, knowing that this meant the end of their dangerous fugitive way of life. He probably expected to be rewarded for bringing such good news, but he obviously didn't know the heart of David. In David's eyes, Saul was never his enemy (2 Sam. 22:1); and on the two occasions when David might have slain Saul, he made it clear that he would never lay hands on the Lord's anointed (1 Sam. 24:1-7; 26:1-11).

The messenger claimed that he was an Amalekite, the son of a resident alien (2 Sam. 1:13). But if he had been living in the land of Israel, he surely would have known that the king of Israel was the anointed of the Lord. If a loyal Jew had found the four corpses, he would have sought to hide them and protect them from the enemy; but the Amalekites were the enemies of Israel, the very people Saul was supposed to wipe out (1 Sam. 15). It's likely that the messenger was a genuine Amalekite but not a resident alien in Israel. He was more likely a "camp follower" who made his living scavenging after the Philistine army. By claiming to be the son of a resident alien, the man was asking for certain privileges specified in the Law of Moses, privileges he certainly didn't deserve (Ex. 22:21; 23:9; Lev. 19:33; 24:22; Deut. 24:17).

A righteous judgment (2 Sam. 1:13-16). At evening, when the time of mourning had ended, David further interrogated the messenger and concluded that the man deserved to die. If the story he told was true, then the man had murdered God's anointed king and deserved to die. If the story was not true, the fact that the Amalekite fabricated a tale about killing the king revealed the depravity of his heart. "Out of your own mouth I will judge you" (Luke 19:22 NKJV). The Jews had been commanded to annihilate the Amalekites (Ex. 17:8-16; Deut. 25:17-19), so when David ordered the messenger to be slain, he was simply obeying the Lord, something Saul had failed to do (1 Sam. 15).

In slaying the messenger, David vindicated Saul and his sons and demonstrated publicly that he had not been Saul's enemy and did not rejoice at Saul's death. This was a dangerous thing to do, for David and his men were living in Philistine territory, and the Philistine king still thought David was his friend and ally. For David to take his stand with the dead king of Israel could be considered an act of treason. But the Lord had vindicated David and David had vindicated Saul, and David wasn't afraid. The conduct of David and his camp, when reported to the Jewish people, would help to convince them that David indeed was chosen by God to be their king.

2. Lamentation (2 Sam. 1:17-27)

David's grief over the death of Saul and Jonathan was sincere, and to help the people remember them, he wrote a touching elegy in their honor. He ordered this lament to be taught and sung in his ancestral tribe of Judah, and no doubt people in other tribes learned and appreciated it. The people of the East unashamedly display their emotions, and their poets frequently write songs to help them commemorate both joyful and painful experiences. Moses taught Israel a song to warn them about apostasy (Deut. 32), and the prophets often wrote funeral dirges to announce impending judgment (Isa. 14:12ff; Ezek. 27:1ff; 28:11-19).

This lament came to be known as "The Song of the Bow" (v. 18)[4] and was recorded in the Book of Jasher (Josh. 10:12-13), a collection of poems and songs that commemorated great events in the history of Israel. "How are the mighty fallen" is the major theme of the elegy (vv. 19, 25, 27), and the emphasis is on the greatness of Saul and Jonathan even in defeat and death. David celebrated their skill and bravery and their willingness to give their lives for their country. Like Hebrews 11, nothing is recorded in the song that speaks of any sins or mistakes in the lives of Saul and Jonathan.

He addresses the people of Israel (2 Sam. 1:19-20). David calls the dead king and his army "Your glory, O Israel" and "the mighty."[5] They didn't display much glory or might in the battle of Gilboa, but Saul was still God's chosen leader and his soldiers were the army of the Lord of Hosts. We're prone to forget that Saul and his army had risked their lives to fight and win many significant battles (1 Sam. 14:47-48) and that the Jewish women did sing "Saul has slain his thousands" (1 Sam. 18:7). David urged the people not to spread the bad news of Israel's defeat, for the Philistines would take care of that. Gath was the capital city of the Philistines where the leaders would rejoice at their victory, and Ashkelon was the chief religious center, where the people would give thanks to their idols for helping their army defeat Israel.

He addresses the mountains of Gilboa (2 Sam. 1:21). This is where the battle was fought and Saul was defeated (2 Sam. 1:6; 1 Sam. 28:4; 31:1). David prayed that God would forsake the place and not send rain or dew to the fields or give the farmers fruitful harvests, even though this meant there could be no grain offerings for the Lord. He asked that God's creation join him in mourning over the defeat of Israel and the fall of their king. When David referred to the shield, was he speaking literally or metaphorically, or both? Saul carried a shield, and Israel's king was compared to a shield (Ps. 84:9; 89:18). Warriors did anoint their leather shields to preserve them, but the king was also God's anointed leader. Saul and his three sons had lost their shields and their lives, and their shields were defiled by blood.

He praises Saul and Jonathan (2 Sam. 1:22-23). This is the heart of the song, depicting Saul and Jonathan as victorious warriors. Jonathan's arrows hit their mark and Saul's sword "did not return unsatisfied."[6] They were as swift as eagles (Deut. 28:49) and as strong as lions (2 Sam. 17:10). But to David, these men weren't just great soldiers; they were also gracious people who were beloved in life and in death loyal to each other and to the people. From his meeting with Samuel in the medium's house, Saul knew that he and his sons would die that day in battle (1 Sam. 28:19), yet he entered the contest determined to do his best. Jonathan knew that his father had disobeyed God and sinned against David, yet he stayed at his side in the fight. Even though the army of Israel was defeated, David wanted the people to remember the greatness of their king and his sons.

He addresses the daughters of Jerusalem (2 Sam. 1:24). In spite of his faults and failures, during his reign Saul had brought stability to the nation. The tribes had abandoned selfish independence and competition and were striving to work together to better their lot, including their economic position. Saul's victories over enemy nations, greater safety in the towns and farmlands, and tribal cooperation all combined to make Israel wealthier. David seems to be describing the wealthy women and their luxuries, perhaps the wives of some of Saul's officers David had seen while he was serving in Saul's court. "Clothed . . . in scarlet and finery" is a familiar phrase that means "basking in wealth."

He speaks to his beloved friend Jonathan (2 Sam. 1:25-26). It's common in funeral dirges to name and address the deceased. "Jonathan my brother" carries a double meaning, for they were brothers-in-law (David was married to Michal, Jonathan's sister) and also brothers in heart and spirit. David and Jonathan were beloved friends who had covenanted together to share the throne, David as king and Jonathan as second in command (1 Sam. 23:16-18). To read homosexual overtones into David's expressions of his love for Jonathan is to misinterpret his words. Solomon described the love of husband and wife as "strong as death" (Song 8:6 NKJV), and the friendship of David and Jonathan was that strong. First Samuel 18:1 NIV says, "Jonathan became one in spirit with David, and he loved him as himself." David closed his lament by repeating the poignant refrain "How are the mighty fallen" and comparing Saul and Jonathan to weapons of war that had been lost and could never be used again.

In composing and teaching this elegy, David may have had several purposes in mind. For one thing, he gave honor to Saul and Jonathan and taught the people to respect the monarchy. Since Saul was Israel's first king, the people might conclude that all their kings would follow his bad example and possibly ruin the nation, so David sought to strengthen the concept of monarchy. The song also made it clear to everybody that David held no grudges against his father-in-law and sovereign. Finally, David set an example for all of us to follow in paying loving tribute to those who have died in battle to protect their country.

3. Coronation (2 Sam. 2:1-4a)

David was Israel's lawful king and couldn't remain in Ziklag since it was in enemy territory. It's likely that Achish the Philistine king thought that David was still under his authority, but David knew that he must return to his own land and begin to reign over his own people. David was in the habit of seeking the Lord's will when he had to make decisions, either by having Abiathar the priest consult the ephod (1 Sam. 23:9-12) or by asking Gad the prophet to pray to God for a word of wisdom (1 Sam. 22:5).

David was from Judah,[7] so it was logical that he go to live among his own people, but in which city should he reside? God gave him permission to return to Judah and told him to live in Hebron, which was located about twenty-five miles from Ziklag. By moving there, David was back with his own people but still under the shadow of the Philistines. Hebron was important in Jewish history, for near the city was the tomb of Abraham and Sarah, Isaac and Rebecca, and Jacob and Leah. The city was in the inheritance of Caleb, a man of stature in Jewish history (Josh. 14:14). Abigail, one of David's wives, had been married to a Calebite, and David had inherited her property near the wilderness of Maon (1 Sam. 25:2). Hebron was probably the most important city in the southern part of Judah, so David moved there with his men, and they lived in the towns surrounding

Hebron. For the first time in ten years, David and his men were no longer fugitives. His men had suffered with him, and now they would reign with him (see 2 Tim. 2:12).

When David settled in Hebron, his return to Judah was the signal for his people to recognize him as their leader, so the elders of Judah anointed David a second time and made him king (see 1 Sam. 16:13).[8] Had Saul's captain Abner also accepted God's will and submitted to David, a costly civil war would have been averted, but loyalty to the old regime (Abner was Saul's nephew) and a desire to protect his own interests motivated Abner to fight David instead of follow him.

While David was living in Ziklag, volunteers had come to him from the tribes of Benjamin, Gad, and Manasseh (1 Chron. 12:1-22), so he not only had a large and experienced army but also a representation from some of the other tribes. Before long, David would win the allegiance of all the nation of Israel.

In his accession to the throne of Israel, David illustrates the career of Jesus Christ, the Son of David. Like David the shepherd, Jesus came first as a humble servant and was anointed king privately. Like David the exile, Jesus is King today but doesn't yet reign on the throne of David. Like Saul in David's day, Satan is still free to obstruct God's work and oppose God's people. One day, Jesus will return in glory, Satan will be imprisoned, and Jesus will reign in His glorious kingdom (Rev. 19:11–20:6). God's people today faithfully pray "Thy kingdom come" (Matt. 6:10 KJV) and eagerly await the return of their King.

David was thirty years old when the elders of Judah made him their king, and he reigned in Hebron for seven and a half years (2 Sam. 2:11). How blessed were the people of Judah to have such a gifted and godly leader!

4. Appreciation (2 Sam. 2:4b-7)

David was a man with a shepherd's heart who cared about his people (see 2 Sam. 24:17), and one of his first concerns was the fate of Saul and the three sons who died with him. When he asked the leaders of Judah about the burial of the royal family, they told him how the men of Jabesh Gilead had risked their lives to recover the four bodies, burn away the decayed and mutilated flesh, and then bury the bones back at Jabesh (1 Sam. 31:8-13). They remembered how Saul had rescued their city many years before (1 Sam. 11).

Jabesh Gilead was located across the Jordan in the tribe of Gad, and the men who recovered the bodies had to travel northwest and cross the Jordan River to reach Beth Shan, a round trip of perhaps twenty-five miles. It was a courageous endeavor, and David thanked them for their devotion to Saul and to the kingdom of Israel. They had displayed "kindness," and the Lord would show them "kindness and faithfulness." Twenty-five years later, David would disinter the remains of Saul and the sons who died with him and rebury them in their native tribe of Benjamin (2 Sam. 21:12-14)

But David used this occasion as an opportunity to invite the brave men of Jabesh Gilead to cast their lot with him. They had been valiant for Saul, and now they could be valiant for David. Some warriors from Gad had already joined David's army while he was in Ziklag (1 Chron. 12:8-15), affirming their confidence that he was God's anointed king. Unfortunately, the people of Jabesh Gilead didn't choose to submit to David but instead followed Abner and Saul's weak son Ish-Bosheth.

The people of Jabesh Gilead allowed their affection for Saul to blind them to God's plan for the nation. They had a good motive, but they made a bad choice. How often in the history of the church have God's people allowed human affection and appreciation to overrule the will of God! Jesus Christ is King and He deserves our submission, loyalty, and obedience. To put human leaders ahead of God's anointed King is to create division and weakness in the ranks of the Lord's followers and invite multiplied problems for the Lord's people. As Augustine of Hippo said, "Jesus Christ will be Lord of all or He will not be Lord at all."

TWO

David Watches and Waits

"In order to govern," said Napoleon on his deathbed, "the question is not to follow out a more or less valid theory but to build with whatever materials are at hand. The inevitable must be accepted and turned to advantage." If this statement is true, then David was a very effective leader during the seven and a half years he ruled in Hebron. While Joab led the army of Judah, David watched and waited, knowing that the Lord would one day open the way for him to reign as king over all Israel. God called David not only to be the king of His people, but also their shepherd and spiritual leader. David had to wait on God's timing while patiently enduring the consequences of the selfish ambitions and reckless actions of leaders who were motivated by pride and hatred. David learned to build with the materials at hand and to trust God to use disappointments to the advantage of his people.

1. Abner the kingmaker (2 Sam. 2:8-32)
The key actor in this drama was Abner, Saul's cousin and the commander of his army (1 Sam. 14:50). It was Abner who brought David to Saul after David killed Goliath (17:55-58) and

who with Saul pursued David for ten years (26:5ff). Abner was rebuked and humiliated by David when he failed to protect the king (26:13-16) and Abner had no special love for David. The people of Israel honored David above Saul and eventually the nation would learn that David was God's choice as king of Israel. But David already had a commander, Joab, so when David became king, what would happen to Abner? Most of what Abner did during those seven and a half years wasn't for the glory of God or the strengthening of Israel, but for his own self-interest. He was taking care of number one.

Abner rejects David's kingship (vv. 8-11). The people of Judah obeyed God's will and anointed David as their king, but Abner disobeyed the Lord and made Saul's one remaining son Ish-Bosheth the king of "all Israel." Abner knew that David was God's choice, a gifted leader and a brave soldier, but he deliberately rebelled against the Lord and appointed Ish-Bosheth. Israel had asked for a king "like all the nations" (1 Sam. 8:5), and when a king died, the other nations appointed a king's eldest son to succeed him. Three of Saul's sons had died in battle, and Ish-Bosheth was all that remained of the royal family.

Scripture doesn't say much about Ish-Bosheth, but it's clear that he was a weak puppet ruler manipulated by Abner (3:11; 4:1). He was certainly old enough to fight in the army with his father and brothers, but Saul left him home to protect the dynasty. (He was probably also a weak soldier.) Saul and Abner both knew that God had taken the dynasty away from Saul (1 Sam. 13:11-14). Knowing that he and his sons would die in the battle, Saul probably arranged to make his fourth son king. Ish-Bosheth may have been crowned by the general, but he was never anointed by the Lord. He is called Esh-Baal in 1 Chronicles 8:33, which means "man of the Lord." The word "baal" means "lord" and was also the name of a Canaanite deity, so that may be why his name was changed.[1]

Abner took Ish-Bosheth to Mahanaim, on the east side of the Jordan. This was a Levitical city of refuge where he would be safe (Josh. 21:38), and there Abner established a capital for "all

Israel." But it's likely that it took at least five years for Abner to pursuade the tribes (minus Judah) to follow their new king. Ish-Bosheth was crowned at the beginning of David's reign of seven years and six months and was assassinated after reigning only two years over "all Israel." This would have been the last two years of David's reign in Hebron. Ish-Bosheth didn't have a long reign over "all Israel," but everybody knew that Abner was in charge anyway.

There's a modern touch to this scenario, for our political and religious worlds are populated by these same three kinds of people. We have weak people like Ish-Bosheth, who get where they are because they have "connections." We have strong, selfish people like Abner, who know how to manipulate others for their own personal profit. We also have people of God like David who are called, anointed, and equipped but must wait for God's time before they can serve. During more than fifty years of ministry, I have seen churches and other ministries bypass God's chosen men and women and put unqualified people into places of leadership just because they were well-known or had "connections."

Abner got what he wanted, but within a few years, he lost it all.

Abner challenges David's army (vv. 12-17). When Abner made Ish-Bosheth king, he was actually declaring war on David, and he knew it. But by now Abner had all the tribes except Judah behind him and he felt he could easily defeat David in battle and take over the entire kingdom. Confident of victory, Abner called for a contest between the two armies, to be held at the great cistern about twenty-three miles north of Gibeon. This was not unlike the challenge Goliath issued when he called for one of Saul's soldiers to fight him (1 Sam. 17:8-10). But Abner was rebelling against God while David was God's chosen leader!

This is the first time we meet Joab, David's nephew and the commander of his army.[2] The two armies met at the reservoir, and twelve soldiers from the army of Benjamin faced twelve men from Judah—and all twenty-four men were killed! That day the battlefield received a new name—"the field of sharp edges" or "the field of daggers." Joab and Abner wasted no time getting their troops in battle formation, and "The battle that day was very fierce." Abner was defeated that day, a portent of things to come.

Abner kills David's nephew (vv. 18-23). Joab, Abishai, and Asahel were David's nephews, the sons of his sister Zeruiah (see 1 Chron. 2:13-16).[3] Whether on his own initiative or at his brother's orders, Asahel went after Abner, for he knew that slaying the enemy general could mean confusing and scattering the whole enemy army. If Joab commanded the fleet-footed young man to go after Abner, perhaps he was thinking of his own future, for Abner might threaten to take his position as head of the army.

The record makes it clear that Abner had no desire to harm or kill the lad, but Asahel was persistent. First Abner told him to turn aside and take what he wanted from one of the dead enemy soldiers. Then he warned Asahel that if he killed him, this would create a "blood feud" that could cause trouble for years to come. Abner knew Joab and had no desire to begin a possible lifelong family conflict. It was bad enough that Joab and Abner were rival generals. When Asahel refused to give up the chase, the clever Abner killed him by using one of the oldest tricks of the battlefield: he stopped suddenly and allowed Asahel to propel himself right into the end of spear. The butt end of a spear was often sharpened so the spear could be thrust into the ground and be ready for action (1 Sam. 26:7). Asahel fell to the ground and died.[4] Asahel died in the course of battle, even though it appears that Abner had no plans or even desire to kill him.

Abner calls for a truce (vv. 25-32). Asahel's two brothers, Joab and Abishai, must have been following close behind because they took up the pursuit of Abner, no doubt determined to avenge the blood of their brother. But Abner's troops rescued him, and he and the Benjamites retreated to the hill of Ammah. Abner knew he was beaten (vv. 30-31), so he called for a truce. He may have suspected that the death of Asahel would encourage Joab and Abishai to stop fighting and take care of burial. Judah and Benjamin were brothers, both sons of Jacob, and why should brother fight brother? But it was Abner who had initiated the battle, so he had only himself to blame. A scheming man, he had a plan in mind that would give him both armies without having to shed blood.

Joab knew the heart of David, that he wanted unity and peace, not division and war, so he blew the trumpet and stopped his troops from pursuing the enemy. He said to Abner, "God only knows what would have happened if you hadn't spoken, for we would have chased you all night if necessary" (v. 27 NLT). Abner and his men walked all night to return to Mahanaim, and Joab and his army returned to Hebron, stopping at Bethlehem along the way to give Asahel a proper burial. During that all-night march, Joab and Abishai hatched a plot to avenge the death of their brother.

2. Abner the negotiator (2 Sam. 3:1-21)

The phrase "a long war" (vv. 1, 6) suggests a state of hostility for two years, occasional clashes rather than one long battle after another. David was biding his time, knowing that God would keep His promises and give him the throne of Israel. David's government in Hebron was going from strength to strength (Ps. 84:7), while the alliance of tribes under Ish-Bosheth and Abner was getting weaker. However, the astute Abner was using his position in the house of Saul to strengthen his own authority, for he was getting ready to make David an offer the king couldn't resist (v. 6).

As for David, his family was also increasing (see also 1 Chron. 3:1-4), and the king now had a growing harem like any other eastern monarch. Of course, David's son Solomon would go far beyond what his father had done or what any Jewish king would do (1 Kings 11:3).[5] David had moved to Hebron with two wives, and now he had six sons by six different wives. Polygamy started with Lamech, a descendant of Cain (Gen. 4:19), and was tolerated in Israel; but it was forbidden to Israel's kings (Deut. 17:17).

Amnon, David's firstborn, would rape his half sister Tamar (chap. 13) and be murdered by Tamar's full brother Absalom, who would be killed while trying to take the kingdom from his father (chap. 14-18). The fact that Absalom was related to royalty on his mother's side might have encouraged his crusade for the kingdom. No doubt David's marriage to Maacah was politically motivated so that David would have an ally near Ish-Bosheth. Chileab is called Daniel in 1 Chronicles 4:1. During David's final illness, Adonijah would try to capture the throne and would be executed by Solomon (1 Kings 1–2). We know nothing about Shephatiah and his mother Abitai, and Ithream and his mother Eglah. After relocating his capital in Jerusalem, David took even more wives and concubines and had eleven more sons born to him (5:13-16).

Abner defects to David (vv. 6-11). Abner was a pragmatic politician as well as a shrewd general, and his basic principle was, "Always join the winning side." When he perceived that the throne of Ish-Bosheth had no future, he decided to switch loyalties and thereby guarantee his own security and possibly save lives. David had a reputation for kindness, and he had shown remarkable patience with the house of Saul.

We aren't told that Abner actually had intercourse with Saul's concubine Rizpah, and he firmly denied it; but if he did, he committed a very serious offense. A deceased king's harem belonged to his successor, in this case, Ish-Bosheth (see 12:8 and 16:15-23), and any man who even asked for one of those women was asking for the kingdom and guilty of treason. This is what led to the death of Adonijah (1 Kings 2:13-25). It's possible that Abner did take Rizpah just to precipitate a quarrel with Ish-Bosheth and to declare his change of allegiance. If so, he succeeded. Of course, the king wasn't strong enough to oppose Abner, who now announced that he was on David's side. The phrase "throne of David" is used in verse 10 for the first time in Scripture, and as time passes, it will take on Messianic significance (Isa. 9:6-7).

Abner negotiates for David (vv. 12-21). This episode is a good example of ancient "shuttle diplomacy."

- Abner sent messengers to David offering to bring all Israel under his rule (v. 12).

- David sent messengers to Abner accepting his offer, provided Abner first sent Michal to him. She was David's wife and Ish-Bosheth's sister (v. 13).
- Abner told Ish-Bosheth to honor David's request, and David also sent Ish-Bosheth a message asking that Michal be sent to Hebron (v. 14).
- Abner conferred with the elders of Israel (vv. 17-18).
- Abner conferred with the leaders of Benjamin (v. 19).
- Abner and twenty representatives from the tribes came to Hebron, bringing Michal with them (vv. 15-16, 20).
- Abner and David agreed on how to transfer the kingdom, and they shared a feast and made a covenant (v. 21).

In the early stages of these negotiations it would have been dangerous and unwise for David and Abner to meet personally, so they depended on their officials to make the necessary contacts. David had no reason not to cooperate with Abner since he had never personally been at war with him or King Saul. Outright war was the only alternative to this kind of diplomacy, and David was a man of peace. David had married into Saul's family, so he had to show some respect both to Abner and Ish-Bosheth, and he was determined to unite the tribes as quickly as possible and with the least amount of bloodshed. He had waited over seven years, and it was time to act.

Why did David make the return of Michal a condition for further negotiation? First of all, she was still his wife, even though Saul had given her to another man. Ten years before, when they were wed, Michal loved David very much (1 Sam. 18:20), and we have reason to believe that David loved her. It was good diplomacy to invite his "queen" to join with him, and the fact that she came from the house of Saul helped to strengthen the bonds of unity. By claiming the daughter of Saul, David was also claiming all the kingdom; and when Abner brought Michal to Hebron, it was a public announcement that he had broken with the house of Saul and was now allied with David.

3. Abner the victim (2 Sam. 3:22-39)

It looked as though everything was in good order for a peaceful transition, but there were hidden land mines in the diplomatic field and they were ready to explode. Ish-Bosheth was still on the throne and David would have to deal with him and the loyal supporters of the house of Saul. Abner had killed Asahel, and Joab was biding his time until he could avenge his brother's death.

Joab reproaches David (vv. 22-25). David had sent Joab and some of his men on a raid to secure wealth to help support the kingdom. On his return, when Joab heard that David had received Abner and given him a feast, his anger erupted and he rebuked the king.[6] The key idea in this paragraph is that Saul's general and the man who killed young Asahel had come and gone "in peace" (vv. 21-23), and Joab couldn't understand it. His own heart was still pained at the death of his brother, and Joab couldn't understand his sovereign's policies. Of course, Joab was protecting his own job just as Abner was protecting his, but unlike David, Joab didn't have any faith in what Abner said or did. Joab was certain that Abner's visit had nothing to do with turning the kingdom over to David. The wily general was only spying out the situation and getting ready for an attack.

The text records no reply from David. Joab had never been easy to deal with (3:39), and the fact that he was a relative made the situation even more difficult. The dynamics of David's family—the multiplied wives, the many children and various relatives in places of authority—created endless problems for the king, and they weren't easy to solve. David's silence wasn't that of agreement, because he didn't agree with his general; it was the silence of restraint and the evidence of a deep desire to put the nation back together again. David wasn't promoting "peace at any price," because he was a man of integrity; but he wasn't prepared to let his impetuous general conduct a personal vendetta in the name of the king. The sentiments of Psalm 120 could certainly apply to David's situation at this time.

Joab deceives Abner and kills him (vv. 26-27). Joab accused Abner of being a liar (v. 25) but practiced deception himself!

We're often guilty of the sins we say others commit, and "it takes a thief to catch a thief." Joab must have sent the messengers in the name of the king or Abner would have been more cautious. Abner hadn't seen Joab at the king's house, so he probably assumed that David's general was still away on his raiding expedition. Abner and his brother Abishai (v. 30) were waiting for Abner, took him to a secluded part of the city gate, and stabbed him under the fifth rib, the same place he had stabbed Asahel (2:23).

Everything about the death of Abner was wrong. The two brothers knew what their king wanted, yet they deliberately put their own interests ahead of that of the kingdom. Asahel had been pursuing Abner on the battlefield, so he was another casuality of war; but the death of Abner was murder. Hebron was a city of refuge, a sanctuary where an accused murderer could get a fair trial, but the two brothers never gave the elders in Hebron a chance to hear the case. Abner killed Asahel in self-defense; but when Joab and Abishai killed Abner, it was pure revenge, and Abner never had opportunity to defend himself. Asahel's death occurred in broad daylight where everybody could witness what happened, but Abner was deceived and led into the shadows. Abishai had accompanied David into Saul's camp and had seen him refuse to kill his father-in-law (1 Sam. 26:6ff), so he knew that David would never countenance the murder of Saul's general. We wonder if Abner died thinking that David had been involved in the plot to kill him.

David honors Abner (vv. 28-39). When David heard the news of Abner's death, he immediately disclaimed any part in what his two nephews had done. In fact, he went so far as to call down a curse on the house of Joab, naming some of the plagues that Moses had warned about in the Covenant (Deut. 28:25-29, 58-62). David issued a royal edict that commanded Joab and his army to mourn over Joab and to attend his funeral. The phrase "all the people" is used seven times in vv. 31-37 (KJV) and refers to the men in Joab's army (2:28; 12:29). David commanded them all to tear their garments, put on sackcloth, and weep over the death of a great man, and David himself followed the bier to the place of interment. Because Joab and Abishai were among the official mourners, it's likely that many of the people didn't know that they were the murderers. David didn't call them to trial, and it's likely that his statements in verses 29 and 39 were spoken privately to his inner council. He tried to shield them as much as possible, although they certainly didn't deserve it.

As he did for Saul and Jonathan, David wrote an official elegy to honor the dead general (vv. 33-34, 38). He made it clear that Abner hadn't died because of some foolish act on his part, and he had never been a prisoner at any time in his military career. He had fallen before wicked men who had deceived him. David further honored Abner by burying him in the royal city of Hebron and not taking him back to Benjamin. Later, David said to his confidential servants that Abner was "a prince and a great man." David also appointed Abner's son Jaasiel as chief officer over the tribe of Benjamin.

David's lament for himself in verse 39 was heard by his select "inner circle" and expressed the problems David had with his own family. The word "weak" doesn't suggest that David was not strong enough to be king, but rather that he was "restrained and gentle" in contrast to the "hard" approach of his nephews. David had experienced God's gentleness (22:36), and he tried to deal with others as God had dealt with him. He no doubt went too far in this approach when it came to his own family (18:5, 14), but David was a man after God's own heart (Ps. 103:8-14). All David could do was leave the judgment with the Lord, for He never makes a mistake.

4. Ish-Bosheth the loser (2 Sam. 4:1-12)

If David thought he was weak because of the behavior of his nephews, he should have considered the situation of Ish-Bosheth following the death of Abner. David was at least a great warrior and a gifted leader, while Ish-Bosheth was a mere puppet in the hands of his general, and now the general was dead. The people of the tribes in his kingdom knew that Abner's death meant the end of the reign of their king, and they no doubt expected a swift invasion by David and his army. The common people knew nothing of David's intentions or of his recent meeting with Abner. It was a day of distress for Ish-Bosheth and his people.

The account of Baanah and Rechab reminds us of the Amalekite in 2 Samuel 1, the man who claimed he killed Saul. These two men were minor officers in Abner's army who thought they could earn rewards and promotion from David if they killed Ish-Bosheth, and like the Amalekite, they were wrong. The only living heir to Saul's throne was a crippled twelve-year-old boy named Mephibosheth, so if Baanah and Rechab killed the king, the way would be open for David to gain the throne and unite the nation. (We will meet Mephibosheth again in 9:1-13; 16:1-4; 19:24-30; and 21:7-8.)

Their excuse for entering the king's house was to secure grain for their men, and while the king was asleep and unprotected, they killed him. If the murder of Abner was a heinous crime, this murder was even worse; for the man's only "crime" was that he was the son of Saul! He had broken no law and injured no person, and he wasn't given opportunity to defend himself. His murderers didn't even show respect to his dead body, for they beheaded him so they could take the evidence to David and receive their reward. Even worse, the two murderers told David that the Lord had avenged him!

David's answer made it clear that at no time in his career had he ever broken God's commandment by murdering somebody in order to accomplish his purposes. The Lord had watched over him and protected him during ten years of exile and now more than seven years as king in Hebron. As when Saul and Abner died, David made it very clear that he was not involved in any way. It would have been very easy for David's enemies to start slanderous rumors that the king had engineered both deaths in order to clear the way for ascending the throne of Israel.

At the king's command, his guards killed the two confessed murderers, cut off their hands and feet, and hung their corpses up as evidence of the king's justice. To mutilate a corpse in this way and then expose it publicly was the ultimate in humiliation (Deut. 21:22-23). David had the head of Ish-Bosheth buried in Hebron in the sepulchre of Abner, for they were relatives.

The four "kings" that Paul wrote about in Romans 5 were certainly active in these scenes from David's life. Sin was reigning (5:21) as men lied to each other, hated each other, and sought to destroy each other. Death also reigned (5:14, 17) as Asahel, Abner, and Ish-Bosheth were slain, along with nearly four hundred soldiers who died at the battle of the pool of Gibeon. But God's grace also reigned (5:21), for He protected David and overruled men's sins to accomplish His divine purposes. "Where sin abounded, grace did much more abound" (5:20 KJV). But David "reigned in life" (5:17) and let God control him as he faced one emergency after another. He was a man empowered by God, and God brought him through each crisis and helped him to succeed.

In the midst of today's troubles and trials, God's people can "reign in life by Jesus Christ" if we will surrender to Him, wait on Him, and trust His promises.

THREE

David, King of Israel

What a remarkable and varied life David lived! As a shepherd, he killed a lion and a bear, and these victories prepared him to kill the giant Goliath. David served as an attendant to King Saul and became a beloved friend of Saul's son Jonathan. For perhaps ten years, David was an exile in the wilderness of Judea, hiding from Saul and learning to trust the Lord more and more. He had patiently waited for the Lord to give him the promised throne, and now that time had come. It is through faith and patience that God's people inherit what He has promised (Heb. 6:12), and David had trusted God in the most difficult circumstances. David inherited a divided people, but with God's help he united them and built Israel into a strong and powerful kingdom. These chapters describe the steps David took to unite and strengthen the nation.

1. David accepted the crown (5:1-5)

The assassination of Ish-Bosheth left the eleven tribes without a king or even an heir to Saul's throne. Abner was dead, but he had paved the way for David to be made king of all twelve tribes (3:17-21). The next step was for the leaders of all the tribes to convene at Hebron and crown David king.

The qualifications for Israel's king were written in the Law of Moses in Deuteronomy 17:14-20. The first and most important requirement was that he was to be chosen by the Lord from the people of Israel, a king "whom the Lord your God chooses" (17:15, 20 NKJV). The people knew that Samuel had anointed David king some twenty years before and that it was God's will that David ascend the throne (2 Sam. 5:2). The nation needed a shepherd, and David was that shepherd (Ps. 78:70-72). Saul had been "the people's king" but he wasn't the Lord's first choice, for God had given him as a judgment against Israel because they wanted to be like the other nations (1 Sam. 8; Hos. 13:11). The Lord loved His people and knew they needed a shepherd, so He equipped David to be their king. Unlike Saul, who was a Benjamite, David was from the royal tribe of Judah (Gen. 49:10) and was born and raised in Bethlehem. Because of this, he was able to establish the dynasty that brought the Messiah Jesus Christ into the world, and He too was born in Bethlehem.

The people who gathered at Hebron reminded David that he belonged to the whole nation and not just to the tribe of Judah (2 Sam. 5:1). At the beginning of David's career, the people recognized that God's hand was upon him, for God gave him success in his military exploits. Present at Hebron were representatives from all the tribes, and they enthusiastically gave their allegiance to the new king (1 Chron. 12:23-40). The total number of officers and men is 340,800, all of them loyal to David. The people remained with David for three days and celebrated God's goodness to His people.[1]

The foundation of the Jewish nation was God's covenant with His people as expressed in the Law of Moses, especially Deuteronomy 27–30 and Leviticus 26. If the king and the people obeyed God's will, He would bless and care for them; but if they disobeyed and worshiped false gods, He would discipline them. Each new king was required to affirm the supremacy and authority of God's law, promise to obey it, and even make a copy of it for his own personal use (Deut. 17:18-20). David entered into a covenant with the Lord and the people, agreeing to uphold and obey God's law and to rule in the fear of the Lord (see 1 Sam. 10:17-25; 2 Kings 11:17).

When David was a teenager, Samuel had anointed him privately (1 Sam. 16:13), and the elders of the tribe of Judah had anointed him when he became their king at thirty years of age (2 Sam. 2:4). But now the elders of the whole nation anointed David and proclaimed him as their king. David was not an amateur, but a seasoned warrior and a gifted leader who obviously had the blessing of the Lord on his life and ministry. After experiencing years of turbulence and division, the nation at last had a king who was God's choice and the people's choice. God takes time to prepare His leaders, and much to be pitied is the person who "succeeds" before he or she is ready for it.

2. David established a new capital city (5:6-10; 1 Chron. 11:4-9)
Abner and Ish-Bosheth had established their capital at Mahanaim (2:8), over the Jordan River on the boundary of Gad and Manasseh, while David's capital was at Hebron in the tribe of Judah. But neither city was suitable for a new ruler who was seeking to unify the nation and make a new beginning. David wisely chose as his capital the Jebusite city of Jerusalem on the border of Benjamin (Saul's tribe) and Judah (David's tribe). Jerusalem had never belonged to any of the tribes, so nobody could accuse David of playing favorites in setting up his new capital.

Political considerations were important, but so was security, and the topography of Jerusalem made it an ideal capital city. Built on a rocky hill and surrounded on three sides by valleys and hills, the city was vulnerable only on the north side. The Valley of Hinnom lay on the south, the Kidron Valley on the east, and the Tyropean Valley on the west. "Beautiful for situation, the joy of the whole earth, is mount Zion, on the sides of the north, the city of the great King" (Ps. 48:2 KJV). "Out of Zion, the perfection of beauty, God hath shined" (Ps. 50:2 KJV). The Jewish people have always loved the city of Jerusalem, and today it is revered by Jews, Christians, and Muslims. To be born in

Jerusalem was a high honor indeed (Ps. 87:4-6).

The Lord must have guided David in a special way when he chose Jerusalem to be his capital, because Jerusalem would play a strategic role in the working out of His great plan of salvation. God had promised the Jews that He would appoint a place where they could come to worship Him (Deut. 12:1-7), and He must have revealed to David that Jerusalem was that place. Later, David would purchase property on Zion which would become the site for the temple that his son Solomon would build (2 Sam. 24). The church sees the earthly Jerusalem as a city of legalistic bondage, but the heavenly Jerusalem as a symbol of the covenant of grace in Christ Jesus (Gal. 4:21-31) and the eternal home of Christ's people (Heb. 12:18-24; Rev. 21–22). God has set His King on the throne (Ps. 2:6), and one day He will speak in His wrath and judge those who oppose Him and His truth.

The Jebusites who lived in Jerusalem thought that their citadel was impregnable and that even the blind and the lame could defend it, a boast that made David angry. He knew that the Lord had promised Moses that Israel would conquer all the nations living in Canaan, including the Jebusites (Ex. 23:23-24; Deut. 7:1-2; 20:17), so by faith he planned his attack. He promised that the man who entered the city and subdued it would be the commander of his army, and he even told him how to do it: go up through the water shaft. David's nephew Joab accepted the challenge, captured the city, and became captain of David's troops. Excavations on Mount Zion have revealed a water shaft that would have been difficult but not impossible to climb. David occupied the mount and called the southern part "the City of David." In years following, David and his successors strengthened the fortress by building walls.

The word "millo" (v. 9) means "fullness" and refers to a stone embankment that was built on the southeastern side of the mount to support additional buildings and a wall. Archaeologists have uncovered what they call "a stepped-stone structure," about 1,500 feet long and 900 feet wide, that was a supporting terrace for other structures, and they assume this was the "millo." Both

Solomon and King Hezekiah strengthened this part of Mount Zion (1 Kings 9:15, 24; 11:27; 2 Chron. 32:5). God's blessing was on David and gave him prosperity in everything he undertook for his people.

It was probably at this time that David brought the head of Goliath to Jerusalem as a reminder of God's faithfulness to His people (1 Sam. 17:54).

3. David formed political alliances (5:11-16; 1 Chron. 3:5-9; 14:1-7)

Israel was a small nation that was distinguished from her neighbors by her special covenant relationship with the true and living God (Num. 23:7-10), and the Jews were warned not to form alliances with their neighbors that would compromise their testimony. Unless his successor bore the same name, Hiram was probably just beginning his reign as king of Tyre, for he befriended both David and Solomon during their reigns (1 Kings 5).

It's likely that David's palace was built for him after his successful wars against the Philistines (5:17-25), and this may have been Hiram's way of recognizing David's accession to the throne. No doubt the Phoenician king also appreciated the fact that David had defeated his warlike neighbors the Philistines. From a practical point of view, it was necessary for the Phoenicians to be on good terms with the Jews because Israel could easily block the trade route to Tyre, and the Phoenicians depended on Jewish farmers for their food. (See Acts 12:20.) David interpreted Hiram's kindness as another evidence that the Lord had indeed established him on the throne of Israel.

The mention of David's palace and his alliance with Hiram offered the writer opportunity to mention David's family, the "house" that the Lord was building for him (Ps. 127). Deuteronomy 17:17 prohibited Israel's king from taking many wives, but David seems to have ignored this law, as did Solomon after him (1 Kings 4:26; 11:1-4). At least one of David's wives was a princess (3:3), which suggests that the marriage was for the sake of political alliance, and no doubt there were other similar marriages. This was one way to cement good relationships with other nations.

There are four lists of David's children in Scripture—those born while he reigned in Hebron (2 Sam 3:2-5) and those born after he moved to Jerusalem (5:13-16; 1 Chron. 3:1-9; 14:4-7). His first wife was Saul's daughter Michal (1 Sam. 18:27), who was childless (2 Sam. 6:23). In Hebron, Ahinoam of Jezreel gave birth to Amnon, David's firstborn (2 Sam. 3:2); Abigail the widow of Nabal gave birth to Chileab, or Daniel (2 Sam. 3:3); princess Maacah bore Absalom (3:3) and his sister Tamar (2 Sam. 13:1); Haggith gave birth to Adonijah (3:4); Abital bore Shephatiah (3:4); and Eglah bore Ithream (3:5). In Jerusalem, Bathsheba bore David four children (1 Chron. 3:5): Shimea (or Shammah), Shobab, Nathan, and Solomon. His other wives, who are not named (1 Chron. 3:6-9), bore David Ibhar, Elishama (or Elishua), Eliphelet (or Elpelet), Nogah, Nepheg, Japhia, Elishama, Eliada (or Beeliada, 1 Chron. 14:7), Eliphelet.[2]

David also had children by his concubines, so he had a large family to manage. It's no wonder that some of them got involved in various court intrigues and brought sorrow to the king. The law clearly stated that the king was not to multiply wives, but both David and Solomon ignored this law, and both paid dearly for their disobedience. It's likely that some of the wives, like Maacah, represented alliances that David made with neighboring kings to help guarantee the security of Israel.

4. David defeated the Philistines (5:17-25; 1 Chron. 14:8-17)
As long as David was minding his own business in Hebron, the Philistines thought he was still one of their vassals; but when he became king of the whole nation of Israel, the Philistines knew he was their enemy and they attacked him. It's probable that these attacks occurred before David relocated in Jerusalem, because he and his men went down to "the stronghold" (5:17), the wilderness area where he had lived in the days when Saul was out to kill him (1 Sam. 22:4; 23:13-14).[3] David got word of the approaching Philistine army, quickly maneuvered his soldiers,

and met the invaders in the Valley of Rephaim, just a short distance from Jerusalem.

As he had done before, David sought the mind of the Lord in planning his attack, probably by using the Urim and Thummim, or he may have had the prophet Gad seek the Lord's will. Assured by the Lord that He would give Israel victory, David met the Philistines two miles southwest of Jerusalem, and he forced them to retreat. They left the field so quickly that they left their idols behind, and David and his men burned them. The Philistines were sure the presence of their gods would assure them victory, but they were wrong. David gave God all the glory and called the place Baal-perazim, which means "the Lord who breaks out."

Some commentators believe that the Gadite warriors joined David's army at this time (1 Chron. 12:8-15), and this was probably the occasion when three of David's "mighty men" broke through the Philistine lines and obtained for David water from the Bethlehem well (2 Sam. 23:13-17; 1 Chron. 11:15-19). It took a great deal of faith and courage for them to do this, and what they did was in response to a *desire in David's heart* and not an order from his lips. They obtained the water because they loved their king and wanted to please him. What an example for us to follow!

The Philistines returned to fight David a second time, and David sought the Lord's will a second time. Unlike Joshua after the victory at Jericho (Josh. 6–7), David didn't assume that the same strategy would work again. God gave him a new battle plan, he obeyed it, and the Lord gave him the victory. What was the sound in the tops of the trees? Only the wind? Angels (Ps. 104:4)? God coming to lead His people to victory? The strategy worked and David pursued the enemy all the way from Gibeon to Gezer, a distance of fifteen to twenty miles. By this victory Israel regained the territory that Saul lost in his last battle. In subsequent campaigns, David also took back the cities the Philistines had taken from Saul (2 Sam. 8:1; 1 Chron. 18:1). David had repeated battles with the Philistines, and the Lord gave him one victory after another (2 Sam. 21:15-22).

The people had long recognized that David was a brave and skillful warrior, and these two victories added greater glory to God and honor to His servant. By defeating the Philistines, David gave notice to Israel's enemies that they had better be careful what they did to him and his people.

5. David relocated the holy ark (2 Sam. 6:1-23; 1 Chron. 13:1-13; 15:1–16:3)[4]

The ark of the covenant was to be kept in the Holy of Holies of the tabernacle, for it symbolized the glorious throne of God (Pss. 80:1; 99:1 NIV); but for over seventy-five years, the ark had been absent from the divine sanctuary at Shiloh. The Philistines captured the ark when Eli was judge (1 Sam. 4) and then returned it to the Jews because the Lord sent judgment on the Philistines. First the ark was sent to Beth Shemesh and then was taken to Kiriath Jearim and guarded in the house of Abinadab (1 Sam 5:1–7:1). During the reign of David, there were two high priests, Zadok and Ahimelech (2 Sam. 8:17), and it's possible that one served at the sanctuary, which was in Shiloh and then moved to Gibeon (2 Chron. 1:1-6), while the other ministered at court in Jerusalem. David pitched a tent for the ark in the City of David, but the furnishings in the tabernacle weren't moved to Jerusalem until after Solomon completed the temple (1 Kings 8:1-4; 2 Chron. 5:1-5).

The first attempt (vv. 1-11). Why did David want the ark in Jerusalem? For one thing, he wanted to honor the Lord and give Him His rightful place as King of the nation. But David also had a secret desire in his heart to build a sanctuary for the Lord (see chap. 7; Ps. 132:1-5), and the first step would be to place the ark in the capital city. David knew that the Lord desired a central sanctuary (Deut. 12:5, 11, 21; 14:23-24; 16:2, 6, 11; 26:2), and he hoped the Lord would let him build it. David's dream didn't come true, but he did buy the land on which the temple was built (2 Sam. 24:18ff), and he provided the temple plans and the wealth and materials needed for its construction (1 Chron. 28–29).

Surely there was a political reason as well for moving the ark to Jerusalem, for it symbolized "one nation under God." David involved all the key leaders in the land in planning the event and issued a general invitation to the priests and Levites to come to Jerusalem from all their cities. "So David assembled all the Israelites, from the Shihor River in Egypt to Lebo Hamath [or "the entrance to Hamath"], to bring the ark of God from Kiriath Jearim" (1 Chron. 13:5). Hamath marked the northernmost boundary assigned by God to Israel (Num. 34:8). It was David's hope that past divisions and tribal differences would be forgotten as the people focused on the Lord. The presence of the ark meant the presence of the Lord, and the presence of the Lord meant security and victory.

But one thing was missing: there is no record that David sought the mind of the Lord in this matter. Relocating the ark to Jerusalem seemed a wise idea and everybody was enthusiastic about doing it, but the king didn't follow his usual pattern of asking the Lord for His directions. After all, what pleases the king and the people may not please God, and what doesn't please God will not have His blessing. David's first attempt failed miserably because the Levites didn't carry the ark on their shoulders. God had given specific directions through Moses how the tabernacle was to be erected, dismantled, and transported (Num. 4), and the major pieces of furniture were to be carried on the shoulders of the Levites who descended from Kohath (vv.4:9-20). When they used a new cart drawn by oxen, they were following the pattern of the pagan Philistines (1 Sam. 6), not the pattern given to Moses on Mount Sinai.

The lesson here is obvious: God's work must be done in God's way if it is to have God's blessing. The fact that all the leaders of Israel agreed to use the cart didn't make it right. When it looked like the ark would fall from the cart, Uzzah presumptuously took hold of it to steady it, and he was killed. But God had warned about this in the Law of Moses, and every Israelite surely knew of it (Num. 1:51; 4:15, 20). There's no evidence that Abinadab was a Levite or that his sons Uzzah and Ahio were even qualified to be near the ark, let alone touch it. David quickly had the ark taken into the house of Obed-Edom, who was a Levite (1 Chron. 15:18, 21, 24; 16:5; 26:4-8, 15), and there it remained for three months.

At the beginning of new eras in biblical history, God sometimes manifested His power in judgment to remind the people that one thing had not changed: God's people must obey God's Word. After the tabernacle was erected and the priestly ministry inaugurated, Aaron's sons Nadab and Abihu were struck dead for willfully trying to enter the sanctuary (Lev. 10). When Israel entered the land of Canaan and began to conquer the land, God had Achan executed for disobeying the law and taking loot from Jericho (Josh. 6–7). During the early days of the New Testament church, Ananias and Sapphira were killed for lying to God and His people (Acts 5). Here, at the start of David's reign in Jerusalem, God reminded His people that they were not to imitate the other nations when they served Him, for all they needed to know was in His Word.

The church today needs to heed this reminder and return to the Word of God for an understanding of the will of God. No amount of unity or enthusiasm can compensate for disobedience. When God's work is done in man's way, and we imitate the world instead of obeying the Word, we can never expect the blessing of God. The crowds may approve what we do, but what about the approval of God? The way of the world is ultimately the way of death.

The second attempt (vv. 12-19). When David heard that the presence of the ark was bringing blessing the household of Obed-Edom, he wanted that blessing for himself and his people. The ark belonged in the tent he had erected for it in Jerusalem. Since 1 and 2 Chronicles were written from the priestly viewpoint, the account of the second attempt is much fuller than the record in Samuel (1 Chron. 15:1–16:3). David was now determined to do God's work in God's way, so he sent the Levites on the ten-mile trip to the house of Obed-Edom, and they brought the ark to Jerusalem on their shoulders. To make sure the Lord wouldn't "break through" with another judgment, the Levites paused after their first six steps and the priests offered a bull and a fattened calf. When no judgment fell, they knew God was pleased with what they were doing (1 Chron. 17:26).[5] When the procession reached the tent in Jerusalem, the priests offered fourteen more sacrifices (1 Chron. 15:26).

David danced enthusiastically in worship before the Lord and dressed for the occasion in a priestly linen ephod (v. 14). Later, his wife accused him of shamelessly exposing himself (v. 20), but 1 Chron. 15:27 informs us that he was also wearing a royal robe under the ephod. Though he was not from the tribe of Levi, David was acting as both king and priest—a picture of Jesus the Son of David, who holds both offices "after the order of Melchizedek" (Heb. 6:20–8:13; Ps. 110). In the days of Abraham, Melchizedek was the king and priest of Salem (Gen. 14:17-24), and now David was worshiping as king and priest of Jerusalem. The procession was accompanied by Levites playing musical instruments and singing songs of praise to the Lord.

David's dance was personal and sincere, and he did it before the Lord as he celebrated the coming of His presence into the capital city. It's probable that some of the psalms (24, 47, 95, 99, 68, 105, 106, 132; see 1 Chron. 16:7-36) reflected his thoughts and feelings on that occasion. In ancient times, dancing played a part in both pagan and Hebrew worship (Ps. 149:3) as well as in the celebrations of special occasions, such as weddings, family gatherings (Luke 15:25), and military victories (Jud. 11:34). Usually it was the women who danced and sang before the Lord (Ex. 15:20-21; 1 Sam. 18:6; Ps. 68:24-26), and on occasions when both men and women danced, they were segregated. Religious dances are mentioned or hinted at in the Book of Psalms (26:6-7; 30:11; 42:4; 150:4).

There is no New Testament evidence that dancing as a "worship art form" was used either in the Jewish synagogue or the liturgy of the early church. The Greeks introduced dancing into worship in the post-Apostolic church, but the practice led to serious moral problems and was finally banned. It was difficult for congregations to distinguish between "Christian dances" and dances honoring a pagan god or goddess, so the church abandoned the practice and later church fathers condemned it.

When the ark was safely installed in the tent, David blessed the people (another priestly act) and gave each person some bread and flesh (or wine) and a cake of raisins. Once again we're reminded of the priest-king Melchizedek, who came from Salem and gave Abraham bread and wine (Gen. 14:18-19). But when David went home to bless his own family, he discovered that his wife was ashamed of him and even despised him for dancing so enthusiastically in public (vv. 16, 20-23). It's interesting that the text says that she saw "King David" and not "her husband" (v. 16) and that she is called "the daughter of Saul" and not "David's wife" (v. 20). When she spoke to him, Michal used the third person ("How glorious was the king") and not the more personal second person, and her speech was very sarcastic. How sad that David's day of happy celebration ended with this kind of insensitive and heartless reception from his own wife, but often God's servants go quickly from the glory of the mountain to the shadows of the valley.

There's no evidence that David was guilty of any of the things his wife accused him of doing. He was properly attired and certainly didn't expose himself to the people, and his dance was before the Lord, who knew what was in his heart. David recognized in Michal the pride and spiritual blindness of her father Saul, whose one desire was to gain and keep his popularity with the people. David preferred to live and serve so as to please the Lord. He reminded Michal that the Lord had chosen him to replace her father as king and that he would do what the Lord prompted him to do. In other words, David didn't need the spiritual counsel of the carnal daughter of a deposed and disgraced king. Perhaps Michal didn't like what David said about her father's neglect of the ark (1 Chron. 13:3). David loved Michal and wanted her back when he became king (3:12-16), but love can easily be bruised when we least expect it.

Michal said that David had disgraced himself before the people, but David countered her false accusation with a declaration that she would be disgraced even more, and from that day on he ignored his marriage duties toward her. For a wife to bear no children was a disgrace in that day, especially if her husband rejected her. But Michal's barrenness was a blessing from the Lord. It prevented Saul's family from continuing in Israel and therefore threatening the throne of David. David and Jonathan had covenanted to reign together (1 Sam. 23:16-18), but God rejected that plan by allowing Jonathan to be slain in battle. The Lord wanted the line and throne of David to be kept apart from any other dynasty, because David's line would culminate in the birth of the Messiah, Jesus Christ. That will be the theme of the next chapter in David's story.

FOUR

David's Dynasty, Kindness, and Conquests

In these four chapters we see King David involved in four important activities: accepting God's will (chap. 7), fighting God's battles (chap. 8), sharing God's kindness (chap. 9) and defending God's honor (chap. 10). However, these activities were nothing new to David, for even before he was crowned king of all Israel he had served the Lord and the people in these ways. Wearing a crown and sitting on a throne didn't change David, for in his character and conduct he had lived like a king all his young life. How tragic that from chapter 11 on, we see David disobeying the Lord and suffering the painful consequences of his sins. Andrew Bonar was correct when he said, "We must be as watchful after the victory as before the battle."

1. Accepting God's will (2 Sam. 7:1-29; 1 Chron. 17:1-27)
In the ancient world, what did kings do when they had no wars to fight? Nebuchadnezzar surveyed his city and boasted, "Is not this great Babylon, that I have built?" (Dan. 4:30). Solomon collected wealth and wives, entertained foreign guests, and wrote books, while Hezekiah seems to have supervised scholars who copied and preserved the Scriptures (Prov. 25:1). But it appears

from 2 Samuel 7:1-3 that in David's leisure hours, the king thought about the Lord and conferred with his chaplain Nathan about improving the spiritual condition of the kingdom of Israel. David wasn't simply a ruler; he was a shepherd with a heart concern for his people. In rest, he thought of work he could do, and in success he thought of God and His goodness to him.

In this chapter, the Lord revealed to Nathan and David what is usually called the Davidic Covenant.[1] This declaration not only had great meaning for David in his day, but it has significance today for Israel, the church, and the world at large.

What the covenant meant to David (vv. 1-9). That David wanted to build a house for the Lord doesn't surprise us, because David was a man after God's own heart and longed to honor the Lord in every possible way. During his years of exile, David had vowed to the Lord that he would build Him a temple (Ps. 132:1-5), and his bringing the ark to Jerusalem was surely the first step toward fulfilling that vow. Now it troubled David that he was living in a comfortable stone house with cedar paneling while God's throne was in a tent, and he shared his burden with Nathan.

This is the first appearance of Nathan in Scripture. Gad had been David's prophet during his exile (1 Sam. 22:5), and after David's coronation, Gad didn't pass from the scene (2 Sam. 24:1-18). In fact, he and Nathan worked together keeping the official records (1 Chron. 29:25, 29) and organizing the worship (2 Chron. 29:25), but Nathan seems to have been the prophetic voice of God to David during his reign. It was Nathan who confronted David about his sin (chap. 12) and also who saw to it that Solomon was crowned king (1 Kings 1:11ff). David had four sons by Bathsheba and named one of them Nathan (1 Chron. 3:1-5).[2] When Nathan told David to do what was in his heart, he wasn't affirming that David's desires were actually God's will. Rather, he was encouraging the king to pursue his desires and see what the Lord wanted him to do. God answered by giving Nathan a special message for the king, and Nathan faithfully delivered it.

In the first part of the message, God reminded David that at no time had He ever asked any tribe or tribal leader to build Him a house. God had commanded Moses to make a tabernacle for His dwelling, and He had been satisfied to travel with His pilgrim people and dwell with them wherever they camped. Now that Israel was in the land and had peace, they needed a caring leader, not a temple, and that's why God called David to shepherd the people of Israel. God had been with David to protect his life and prosper his service and had made David's name great. In spite of his desires and his oath, David would not build the temple. The best thing he could do for the Lord was to continue shepherding the people and setting a godly example.

This announcement must have disappointed David, but he accepted it graciously and gave the Lord thanks for all His goodness to him. When Solomon dedicated the temple, he explained that God accepted David's desire for the deed: "Whereas it was in your heart to build a house for My name, you did well that it was in your heart" (1 Kings 8:18 NKJV; see 2 Cor. 8:12). God's servants must learn to accept the disappointments of life, for as A. T. Pierson used to say, "Disappointments are His appointments."

What the covenant means to Israel (vv. 10-15). The foundation for God's purposes and dealings with the people of Israel is His covenant with Abraham (Gen. 12:1-3; 15:1-15). God chose Abraham by His grace and promised him a land, a great name, multiplied descendents, and His blessing and protection. He also promised that the whole world would be blessed through Abraham's seed, and this refers to Jesus Christ (Gal. 3:1-16). God called Israel to be the human channel through which His Son and His Word would come to the world. God's covenant with David builds on this covenant with Abraham, for it speaks about the nation, the land, and the Messiah.

The Lord began with the subject of Israel's land (v. 10) and promised "rest" to His people. The word "rest" is an important word in the prophetic vocabulary and refers to a number of blessings in the plan of God for His people. The concept of "rest" began with God's rest when He completed creation (Gen. 2:1-3), and this was a basis for Israel's observance of the Sabbath (Ex. 20:8-11). After God delivered Israel from Egypt, He promised them "rest" in their own land (Ex. 33:14; Deut. 25:19; Josh. 1:13, 15). David was so busy fighting wars that he couldn't build the temple (1 Kings 5:17),[3] but when God gave rest to Israel, Solomon built the temple using the plans and materials that God gave his father David (1 Kings 5:1-4; 8:56; Ps. 89:19-23).

But the concept of "rest" goes beyond any of these matters because it speaks also of the spiritual rest that believers have in Christ (Matt. 11:28-30; Heb. 2:10-18; 4:14-16). The concept also looks ahead to Israel's future kingdom and the rest that God's people will then enjoy when Jesus Christ sits upon David's throne (Isa. 11:1-12; 65:17-25; Jer. 31:1-14; 50:34).

Then the Lord turned from promises concerning the land and the nation to promises concerning David's throne and family (vv. 11-16). Every king is concerned about the future of his kingdom, and the Lord promised David something above and beyond anything he could have imagined. David wanted to build God a house (the temple), but God promised to build David a house—a dynasty forever! The word "house" is used fifteen times in this chapter and refers to David's palace (vv. 1-2), the temple (vv. 5-7, 13), and David's dynasty, culminating in Messiah, Jesus Christ (vv. 11, 13, 16, 18-29).

God's first announcement of the coming of the Savior was given in Genesis 3:15, informing us that the Savior would be a human being and not an angel. Genesis 12:3 tells us that He would be a Jew who would bless the whole world, and Genesis 49:10 that He would come through the tribe of Judah. In this covenant, God announced to David that Messiah would come through his family, and Micah 5:2 prophesied that He would be born in Bethlehem, the City of David (see Matt. 2:6). No wonder the king was so elated when he learned that Messiah would be known as "the Son of David" (Matt. 1:1)!

In this section, the Lord speaks about Solomon as well as about the Savior, who is "greater than Solomon" (Matt. 12:42). Solomon would build the temple David longed to build, but his reign would end; however, the reign of Messiah would go on forever. David would have a house forever (vv. 25, 29), a kingdom forever (v. 16), and a throne forever (vv. 13, 16), and would glorify God's name forever (v. 26).

All of this is fulfilled in Jesus Christ, the Son of David (Ps. 89:34-37; Luke 1:32-33, 69; Acts 2:29-36; 13:22-23; 2 Tim. 2:8) and will be manifested when He returns, establishes the promised kingdom, and sits on David's throne. The spiritual blessings God offered to David are today offered in Jesus Christ to all who will trust Him (Isa. 55:1-3; Acts 13:32-39). They will be fulfilled literally by Jesus Chirst in the future kingdom promised to Israel (Isa. 9:1-7; 11:1-16; 16:5; Jer. 33:15-26; Ezek. 34:23-24; 37:24-25; Hos. 3:5; Zech. 12:7-8).[4] The throne of David ended in 586 BC with Zedekiah, the last king of Judah, but the line of David continued and brought Jesus Christ the Son of God into the world (Matt. 1:12-25; Luke 1:26-38, 54-55, 68-79).

Humanly speaking, the nation of Israel would have perished quickly had not God been faithful to His covenant with David, who was "the light [lamp] of Israel" (21:17). No matter to what depths the kings and people descended, the Lord preserved a lamp for David and for Israel (1 Kings 11:36; 15:4; 2 Kings 8:19; 2 Chron. 21:7; Ps. 132:17). Whether they recognized it or not, the Jewish people were heavily indebted to David for their temple, the instruments and songs used in the temple, the organization of the temple ministry, and the protection the nation had from the enemy nations. We today are indebted to David for keeping the light shining so that the Savior could come into the world. In spite of the nation's sins, God chastened His people, but He did not break His covenant or take His mercy away (v. 15; 22:51; 1 Kings 3:6; 2 Chron. 6:42; Ps. 89:28, 33, 49).

What the covenant means to believers today (vv. 18-29). We have already noted that there is a church today because God used David's family to bring the Savior into the world, and there is a future for Israel because God gave David a throne forever. The way that David responded to this great Word from God is a good example for us to follow today. He humbled himself before the Lord and at least ten times called himself the servant of God. Servants usually stand at attention and wait for orders, but David sat before the Lord. The covenant God gave David was unconditional; all David had to do was accept it and let God work. Like a little child speaking to a loving parent, the king called himself "David" (v. 20), and he poured out his heart to the Lord.

First he focused on *the present* as he gave praise for the mercies God bestowed on him (vv. 18-21). It was God's grace that had brought David this far—from the sheepfolds to the throne—and now God had spoken about his descendents far into the future. In verses 18-20 and 28-29, David addressed God as "Lord God," which in Hebrew is "Jehovah Adonai, the Sovereign Lord." (In vv. 22 and 25, it's "Jehovah Elohim," the God of power.) Only a God of sovereign grace would give such a covenant, and only a God with sovereign power could fulfill it. "Do you deal with everyone this way, O Sovereign Lord?" (v. 19 NLT). In one sense, the answer is no, because God chose the house of David to bring His Son into the world; but in another sense, the answer is yes, because any sinner can trust Jesus Christ and be saved and enter into the family of God. David saw the promises of this covenant as a "great thing" (v. 21) because of the dependability of God's Word and God's love.

In verses 22-24, David looked at *the past* and God's amazing grace toward Israel. The Lord chose Israel instead of the other nations on the earth, and He revealed Himself to Israel by giving the law at Mount Sinai and speaking the Word through His prophets. The Jews were to remember the uniqueness of the Lord and not bow before the idols of the other nations. (See Deut. 4:34; 7:6-8; 9:4-5; Neh. 9:10.) God is the Lord of all nations but He did great things for Israel, His chosen people. David recognized the wonderful truth that God had chosen Israel to be His people forever!

The third part of David's prayer and praise (vv. 25-29) looked to *the future* as revealed in the covenant just delivered to the king. God gave the Word, David believed it, and David asked God to fulfill that Word for His people. He wanted Israel to continue as a nation and the Lord to be magnified through Israel. He asked that his house be built just as the Lord had promised (v.

27), even though it was disappointing to David that he wasn't permitted to build a house for the Lord. "Thy kingdom come" is the thrust of verse 27, and "Thy will be done" the thrust of verse 28. It was enough for David simply to hear the promises and believe them; he also prayed to the Lord to fulfill them.

In his humility, faith, and submission to God's will, David is a good example for us to follow.

2. Fighting God's battles (2 Sam. 8:1-18; 1Chron. 18)

This chapter summarizes the victories of the army of Israel over their enemies, events that most likely occurred between chapters 6 and 7 of 2 Samuel (see 7:1). The Lord helped David, Joab, and Abishai to overcome Israel's enemies on the west (v. 1), east (v. 2), north (vv. 3-12), and south (vv. 13-14). For a parallel account, see 1 Chronicles 18-19. King Saul had fought many of these same enemies (1 Sam. 14:47).

We must look at David's military activities in the light of God's covenants with Israel through Abraham (Gen. 12, 15), Moses (Deut. 27–30) and David (2 Sam. 7). The Lord had promised Israel the land from the River of Egypt to the Euphrates River (Gen. 15:17-21; Deut. 1:6-8; 11:24; 1 Kings 4:20-21), and the Lord used David to help fulfill the promise. Israel had lost territory to her enemies during the reign of King Saul, and David recaptured it, but he also expanded Israel's borders and acquired land that hadn't been conquered in Joshua's day (Josh. 13:1-7). David established vassal treaties with most of these nations and set up garrisons in their lands to maintain Israel's authority (v. 6). A man of faith, David believed God's promises and acted upon them for the blessing of his people.

But David's victories also meant peace and safety for the people of Israel so they could live normal lives and not be constantly threatened by their neighbors. Israel had a great work to perform on earth in bearing witness to the true and living God and bringing the written Scriptures and the Messiah into the world. Furthermore, David's victories enriched the treasury of the Lord so that the material was available for Solomon to build the temple (vv. 11-13; 1 Chron. 22). The church today doesn't use military weapons to fight God's battles (John 18:36-38; 2 Cor. 10:3-6; Eph. 6:14-18), but we could use the faith and courage of David and his soldiers and reclaim lost territory for the Lord.

West: the Philistines (v. 1) were the traditional enemies of the Jews and seized every opportunity to attack them. In 2 Samuel 21:15-22, at least four different Philistine campaigns are mentioned (see also 1 Chron. 20:4-8), and the text describes the slaying of several giants as well as the defeating of the Philistines. Israel captured several cities, including Gath, the home of Goliath. As a youth, David had killed Goliath, but during the first campaign he was unable to slay the giant Ishbi-benob, and David's nephew Abishai had to rescue him (21:15-17). David's men advised him to stop waging war personally, and he heeded their advice. Blessed is that leader who admits his weaknesses and admits when he needs to make changes! The name "Methegammah" means "the bridle of the mother city" and probably refers to a key Philistine city that Israel captured, the location of which is a mystery to us. To "take the bridle" of anything means to gain control and force submission.

East: the Moabites (v. 2) had been friendly to David because they thought he was Saul's enemy (1 Sam. 14:47), and David was related to the Moabites through his great-grandmother Ruth (Ruth 4:18-22). While living in exile, David had even put his parents in the custody of the king of Moab (1 Sam. 22:3-4). The Moabites were actually related to the Jews because Abraham's nephew Lot was the father of their ancestor Moab (Gen. 19:30-38). Because the Moabites had hired Balaam the prophet to curse Israel and then led Moab in seducing the men of Israel (Num. 22–25), the Lord declared war on Moab, and David was only continuing that crusade. Most conquerors would have slaughtered the entire army, but David spared every third soldier and settled for tribute from the nation.

North: the Arameans and Syrians (vv. 3-13). Zobah was located north of Damascus and was part of a confederacy of nations called "the Syrians" in some translations, but more accurately they are "the Arameans." However, their neighbors the Syrians tried to come to their rescue and were defeated themselves, so that the whole area north to the Euphrates came under David's authority. This gave Israel important military installations and also control of the valuable caravan routes that passed through that territory. Israel could levy duty as the traders passed through and thereby increase its income. By defeating the Arameans and the Syrians, David also made friends with their enemies and received tribute from them (vv. 6-10).

South: the Edomites (vv. 12-14). First Chronicles18:12-13 names the Edomites as the enemy (see 1 Kings 11:14b-18), but it's possible that the Syrians and Arameans at this time were in control of Edom and were also involved in the battle. It appears that while Israel was attacking the Syrians and Arameans in the north, the Moabites attacked them from the south, but the Lord gave Israel a great victory. Though David and Joab were the conquering leaders in this battle, it was the Lord who received the glory when David commemorated the victory in Psalm 60. "Over Edom I will cast My shoe" (60:8 NKJV) is a metaphorical expression that may have a dual meaning: (1) God claims Edom as His territory, and (2) God treats Edom like a slave who cleans the master's shoes. It expresses the humiliation God brought to the proud Edomites whom David conquered.

David also defeated the Amalekites (v. 12), a commission that his predecessor Saul had failed to fulfill (1 Sam. 15). From the days of Moses, the Lord had declared war on Amalek (Ex. 17:8-12; Num. 14:45; Deut. 25:17-19), and David was only continuing the crusade. Just as the Lord promised (7:9), David was victorious over his enemies. David's reputation increased dramatically because of these victories (v. 13), and David was careful to give God the glory (8:11-12).

Administration in Jerusalem (vv. 15-18).[5] Winning battles is one thing and managing the affairs of the growing nation is quite another, and here David proved himself capable. He ruled with justice and righteousness and served all the people (v. 15). David described such a leader in 23:1-7 and compared him to the sunrise and the sunlight after rain. Certainly David brought the dawning of a new day to Israel after the darkness of Saul's reign, and God used David to bring calm after the storm. God loves righteousness and justice (Ps. 33:5) and manifests both as He rules over His universe (Pss. 36:6; 99:4; Isa. 5:16; Jer. 9:24; Amos 5:24). David indeed was a man after God's own heart.

A good ruler must appoint wise and skilled subordinates, and this David did. David's nephew Joab had treacherously killed Abner (3:27-39), but David made him head of the army. We know little about Jehoshaphat or his position in David's government. The "recorder" ("secretary" NIV) was probably the officer who kept the records and advised the king as would a secretary of state. He may have been the chairman of the king's council. The scenario in Isaiah 36 indicates that the secretary/recorder was a person of high rank (see vv. 3, 22).

Zadok and Ahimelech were both serving as priests, for the ark was in Jerusalem and the tabernacle was at Gibeon (1 Chron. 16:39ff). Ahimelech the priest was slain by Doeg at Saul's command (1 Sam. 22:6ff) and his son Abiathar survived the slaughter of the priests at Nob and joined David's band at Keilah (22:20; 23:6). He accompanied David during his exile years and must have fathered a son whom he named Ahimelech after the boy's martyred grandfather. When he came of age, the boy served with his father and Zadok. You find Zadok and Abiathar working together when the ark was brought to Jerusalem (2 Sam. 15:24, 35) and when Absalom revolted against David (2 Sam. 17:15; 19:11-12).

Seriah the scribe ("secretary" NIV) was also known as Sheva (20:25), Shavsha (1 Chron. 18:16), and Shisha (1 Kings 4:3). The reference in Kings informs us that two of his sons inherited his position. The most remarkable appointment is that of Benaiah, the officer over David's bodyguard and a mighty warrior (23:20-23), who was a priest (1 Chron. 27:5). In the Old Testament, it wasn't unusual for a priest to become a prophet (Jeremiah, Ezekiel), but for a priest to become an army officer was unusual. The Cherethites and Pelethites were exceptional mercenaries from other nations who made up David's personal bodyguard. Benaiah became an invaluable aide to Solomon (1 Kings 1:38, 44).

While not all of David's sons proved to be worthy men, he had them serving as officers in his government. It was not only good for them, but it was one way for him to get information concerning what was going on in the nation. The title "chief rulers" ("royal advisers" NIV) is a translation of the Hebrew word for "priests." Since David belonged to the tribe of Judah, neither he nor his sons could enter the holy precincts of the tabernacle and minister as priests, so the word probably means "confidential advisers." These were men who had access to the king and assisted him in directing the affairs of the kingdom.

3. Sharing God's kindness (2 Sam. 9:1-13)

"The kindness of God" is the one of two themes in this chapter (vv. 1, 3, 7), and it means the mercy and favor of the Lord to undeserving people. Paul saw the kindness of God in the coming of Jesus Christ and His work on the cross (Titus 3:1-7 [3:4]; Eph. 2:1-9 [2:7]), and we see in David's dealings with Mephibosheth a picture of God's kindness to lost sinners. David had promised both Saul and Jonathan that he would not exterminate their descendants when he became king (1 Sam. 20:12-17, 42; 24:21), and in the case of Jonathan's son Mephibosheth, David not only kept his promise but went above and beyond the call of duty.

The second major theme is the kingship of David. The name "David" is used by itself six times in the chapter: six times he's called "the king," and once the two are united in "King David" (v. 5). Nobody in all Israel except David could have shown this kindness to Mephibosheth because David was the king. He had inherited all that had belonged to King Saul (12:8) and could dispose of it as he saw fit. Surely we have here a picture of the Son of David, Jesus Christ, who through His death, resurrection and ascension has been glorified on the throne of heaven and can now dispense His spiritual riches to needy sinners. The name "David" means "beloved," and Jesus is God's beloved Son (Matt. 3:17; 17:5), sent to earth to save lost sinners.

Finding Mephibosheth (vv. 1-4). It's important to note that David's motivation for seeking Mephibosheth was not the sad plight of the crippled man but David's desire to honor Jonathan, the father. He did what he did "for Jonathan's sake" (1 Sam. 20:11-17). Mephibosheth was five years old when his father died in battle (4:4), so he was now about twenty-one years old and had a young son of his own (v. 12). David couldn't show any love or kindness to Jonathan, so he looked for one of Jonathan's relatives to whom he could express his affection. So it is with God's children: they are called and saved, not because they deserve anything from God, but for the sake of God's Son, Jesus Christ (Eph. 1:6; 4:32). God in His grace gives us what we don't deserve, and in His mercy doesn't give us what we do deserve.

David found out where Mephibosheth was living by asking Ziba, who served as an "estate manager" for Saul. Ziba answered David's questions about Mephibosheth, but he turned out to be very deceitful and lied to the king about Mephibosheth when David fled from Absalom (16:1-4) and when David returned to Jerusalem (19:17, 24-30). The combination of David's impulsiveness and Ziba's deceit cost Mephibosheth half his property.

Calling Mephibosheth (vv. 5-8). What were the lame prince's thoughts when the summons came to appear before the king? If he believed what his grandfather had said about David, he would have feared for his life; but if he had listened to what his father told him about David, he would have rejoiced. Someone had to help the young man to the palace, where he fell before David— something difficult for a person with crippled legs—and acknowledge his own unworthiness. The king spoke his name and immediately assured him that there was nothing to fear. David then unofficially "adopted" Mephibosheth by restoring to him the land that his father Jonathan would have inherited from Saul, and then by inviting him to live at the palace and eat at the king's table. David had eaten at Saul's table and it had nearly cost him his life, but Mephibosheth would eat at David's table and his life would be protected.

The fact that David made the first move to rescue

Mephibosheth reminds us that it was God who reached out to us and not we who sought Him. We were estranged from God and enemies of God, yet He loved us and sent His Son to die for us. "But God demonstrates His own love toward us, in that while we were still sinners, Christ died for us" (Rom. 5:8 NKJV). For David to rescue and restore Mephibosheth cost him only the land of Saul, which he had never paid for to begin with; but for God to restore us and bring us into His family, Jesus had to sacrifice His life. Our inheritance is much more than a piece of real estate on earth: it's an eternal home in heaven!

Enriching Mephibosheth (vv. 9-13). David took him into his own family, provided for him, protected him, and let him eat at his own table. It wouldn't be easy to care for a grown man who was lame in both feet, but David promised to do so. Whereas previously Mephibosheth had Ziba and his fifteen sons and twenty servants working for him (v. 10), now all the resources and authority of the king of Israel were at his disposal! Ziba and his sons and servants would still work the land for Mephibosheth and give him the profits, but those profits would be insignificant compared with the king's wealth. David's words "eat at my table" are found four times in the passage (vv. 7, 10, 11, 13) and indicate that Jonathan's son would be treated like David's son.

Mephibosheth looked upon himself as a "dead dog" (v. 8), and we were "dead" in our trespasses and sins when Jesus called us and gave us new life (Eph. 2:1-6). We have a higher position than that which David gave Mephibosheth, for we sit *on the throne* with Jesus Christ and reign in life through Him (Rom. 5:17). God gives us the riches of His mercy and grace (Eph. 2:4-7) and "unsearchable riches" in Christ (Eph. 3:8). God supplies all our needs, not out of an earthly king's treasury, but according to "his riches in glory" (Phil. 4:19). Mephibosheth lived the rest of his life in the earthly Jerusalem (v. 13), but God's children today are already citizens of the heavenly Jerusalem, where they will dwell forever with the Lord (Heb. 12:22-24).

This touching event in the life of David not only illustrates the believer's spiritual experience in Christ, but it also reveals to us that David was indeed a man after God's own heart (1 Sam. 13:14; Acts 13:22). He was a shepherd who had a special concern for the lame sheep in the flock.[6]

One last fact should be noted: when some of Saul's descendants were chosen to be slain, David protected Mephibosheth from death (21:1-11, especially v. 7). There was another descendant named Mephibosheth (v. 8), but David knew the difference between the two! The spiritual application to believers today is obvious: "There is therefore now no condemnation to those who are in Christ Jesus" (Rom. 8:1 NKJV). "For God did not appoint us to wrath, but to obtain salvation through our Lord Jesus Christ" (1 Thes. 5:9 NKJV). "He who believes in Him is not condemned; but he who does not believe is condemned already, because he has not believed in the name of the only begotten Son of God" (John 3:18 NKJV).

Mephibosheth is a difficult name to remember and pronounce, but he reminds us of some wonderful truths about "the kindness of God" shown to us through Jesus Christ our Savior and Lord.

4. Vindicating God's honor (2 Sam. 10:1-19; 1 Chr. 19:1-19)

Once again, David wanted to show kindness, but this time his attempt led to war instead of peace. His overtures to his neighbor were misunderstood, and David had to defend his own honor as well as the honor of the Lord and His people.

A public offense (vv. 1-5). King Saul's first military victory was over Nahash and the Ammonite army when they attacked Jabesh Gilead (1 Sam. 11). Like the Ammonites, the Moabites were descendants of Lot (Gen. 19:30ff) and therefore relatives of the Jews. How did David become friendly with the Ammonites when his predecessor was at war with them? It probably occurred when David was in exile and appeared to be at war with Saul. During those "outlaw years," David tried to build a network of friendships outside Israel that he hoped would help him when he became king. The phrase "show kindness" can carry the meaning of "make a covenant,"[7] so it may have been David's desire not only to comfort Hanun but also to make a treaty with him.

David sent a delegation of court officials to Hanun, but immaturity and ignorance triumphed over wisdom and common sense. The inexperienced new king listened to his suspicious advisers and treated David's men as though they were spies. (Years later, Solomon's son Rehoboam would make a similar mistake and follow unwise counsel. See 1 Kings 12.) The Ammonites shaved the ambassadors' faces, leaving but one side of each beard intact, and then cut the men's official garments off at the waist. Jewish men were supposed to keep their beards intact (Lev. 19:27; 21:5; Deut. 14:1-2), and to tamper with a man's beard was a great insult. All Jews were to be dressed modestly, so exposing the men's bodies was even more embarrassing. It was treating them as though they were prisoners of war (Isa. 20:3-4), and it also meant removing some of the tassels on their garments that identified them as Jews (Deut. 22:12; Num. 15:37-41).

The first battle (vv. 6-14). The members of the delegation could easily secure other garments, but it would take time for their beards to grow; so they stayed in Jericho until they looked presentable. However, new beards couldn't erase old wounds. When King Hunan allowed his officials to mistreat the delegation, he not only insulted the men personally, but he also insulted King David who sent them and the nation they represented. In short, it was a declaration of war.

But King Hunan wasn't prepared for war, especially against a seasoned general like Joab and a famous king like David; so he paid a thousand talents of silver (1 Chron. 19:6) to hire troops from the north, including Syrians and Arameans, nations that David eventually defeated (8:12).[8] These 33,000 soldiers joined with the Ammonite army in attacking the Jewish army. Actually, Joab faced two armies who were using a pincer movement to defeat Israel, with the Syrians and Arameans coming from the north and the Ammonites coming from the south. Joab wisely divided his forces and put his brother Abishai in charge of the southern front, and with the Lord's gracious help, Joab so defeated the northern troops that his victory frightened the southern troops to flee to Rabbath, the fortified capital city of Ammon.

The second battle (vv. 15-19). David came personally to lead the battle against the Syrians,[9] and he and the army of Israel defeated them and the Syrians became vassal states in David's growing empire. Joab wisely waited to set up a siege against the Ammonite capital of Rabbah at that time, so he waited to renew the attack in the spring of the year (11:1). He took the city and David came to finish the siege and claim the honors (12:26-31). It was while Joab and his men were besieging Rabbah that David remained in Jerusalem and committed adultery with Bathsheba.

David indeed was a man of war and fought the battles of the Lord, and the Lord was with him to give him victory. He extended the Israelite empire to the River of Egypt on the south, to the Euphrates River on the north, and on the east he conquered Edom, Moab, and Ammon, and on the north defeated the Arameans and the Syrians, including Hamath. Because of God's gifts and help, David undoubtedly became Israel's greatest king and greatest military genius. He was blessed with courageous men like Joab and Abishai, plus his "mighty men" (2 Sam. 23; 1 Chron. 11:10-47).

FIVE

David's Disobedience, Deception, and Discipline[1]

Unlike the average campaign biography or press release, the Bible always tells the truth about people. It should encourage us to know that even the best men and women in the biblical record had their faults and failures, just as we do, and yet the Lord in His sovereign grace was able to use them to accomplish His purposes. Noah was a man of faith and obedience, and yet he got drunk. Twice Abraham lied about his wife, and Jacob lied to both his father Isaac and to his brother Esau. Moses lost his temper when he struck the rock, and Peter lost his courage and denied Christ three times.

Here we see David, the man after God's own heart, who committed adultery and then murdered a man in a last-ditch effort to cover his own sin. For at least nine months, David refused to confess his sins, but then God spoke to Him and he sought the face of the Lord and made a new beginning. But he paid dearly for his sins for, as Charles Spurgeon said, "God does not allow his children to sin successfully." Alas, David suffered the consequences of his sins for the rest of his life, and so shall we if we rebel against Him, for the Lord chastens those He loves and seeks to make them obedient. The good things that we receive in life, we pay for in advance, for God prepares us for what He has prepared for us. But the evil things we do are paid for on the installment plan; and bitter is the sorrow brought by the consequences of forgiven sin.

These two chapters describe seven stages in David's experience. As we study, let's remember Paul's admonition, "Therefore let him who thinks he stands take heed lest he fall" (1 Cor. 10:12 NKJV).

1. The conceiving (2 Sam. 11:1-3)

David's temptation and sin illustrate the truth of James 1:14-15—"But each one is tempted when he is drawn away by his own desires and enticed. Then, when desire has conceived, it gives birth to sin; and sin, when it is full-grown, brings forth death" (NKJV). It isn't difficult to see how it all developed.

Idleness (vv. 1-2a). The account of David's sins is given against the background of Joab's siege of Rabbah, the key city of the Ammonites (11:1, 16-17; 1 Chron. 20:1-3). The Ammonite army had fled to the walled city of Rabbah (10:14), and Joab and the Israel troops were giving the people time to run out of food and water, and then they would attack. David sent Joab and the troops to lay siege to Rabbah, but he himself remained in Jerusalem. It was probably April or May and the winter rains had stopped and the weather was getting warmer. Chronologists calculate that David was about fifty years old at this time. It's true that David had been advised by his leaders not to engage actively in warfare (2 Sam. 21:15-17), but he could have been with his troops to help develop the strategy and give moral leadership.

Whatever the cause, good or bad, that kept David in Jerusalem, this much is true: "Satan finds some mischief still for idle hands to do."[2] Idleness isn't just the absence of activity, for all of us need regular rest; idleness is also activity to no purpose. When David was finished with his afternoon nap, he should have immediately moved into some kingdom duty that would have occupied his mind and body, or, if he wanted to take a walk, he should have invited someone to walk with him. "If you are idle, be not solitary," wrote Samuel Johnson; "if you are solitary, be not idle." Had David followed that counsel, he would have saved himself and his family a great deal of heartache.

When David laid aside his armor, he took the first step toward moral defeat, and the same principle applies to believers today (Eph. 6:10-18). Without the helmet of salvation, we don't think like saved people; and without the breastplate of righteousness, we have nothing to protect the heart. Lacking the girdle of truth, we easily believe lies ("We can get away with this!"), and without the sword of the Word and the shield of faith, we are helpless before the Enemy. Without prayer we have no power. As for the shoes of peace, David walked in the midst of battles for the rest of his life. He was safer on the battlefield than on the battlement of his house!

Imagination (v. 2b). A man can't be blamed if a beautiful woman comes into his line of vision, but if the man deliberately lingers for a second look in order to feed his lust, he's asking for trouble. "You heard that it was said, You shall not commit adultery," said Jesus. "But as for myself, I am saying to you, Everyone who is looking at a woman in order to indulge his sexual passion for her, has already committed adultery with her in his heart" (Matt. 5:27-28, *Wuest's Expanded Translation*). When David paused and took that longer second look, his imagination went to work and started to conceive sin. That would have been a good time to turn away decisively and leave the roof of his palace for a much safer place. When Joseph faced a similar temptation, he fled from the scene (Gen. 39:11-13). "Watch and pray, lest you enter into temptation. The spirit indeed is willing, but the flesh is weak" (Matt. 26:41 NKJV).

"Lead us not into temptation" was the prayer David should have prayed. By lingering and looking, David tempted himself. By sending the messengers, he tempted Bathsheba; and by yielding to the flesh, He tempted the Lord.

Information (v. 3). When God forbids something and calls it sin, we shouldn't try to get more information about it. "I want you to be wise in what is good, and simple concerning evil"

(Rom. 16:19). David knew what the law said about adultery, so why did he send to inquire about the woman? [3] Because in his heart, he had already taken possession of her, and now he was anxious to have a rendezvous with her. He learned that Bathsheba was a married woman, and that fact alone should have stopped him from going on with his evil plan. When he found out she was the wife of one of his courageous soldiers who was even then on the battlefield (23:9), he should have gone to the tent of meeting, fallen on his face and cried out to God for mercy. From the brief genealogy given, David should have realized that Bathsheba was the granddaughter of Ahithophel, his favorite counselor (23:34; 16:23). No wonder Ahithophel sided with Absalom when he revolted against his father and seized the kingdom!

David knew the law and should have remembered it and applied it to his own heart. "You shall not covet your neighbor's wife" (Ex. 20:17); "You shall not commit adultery" (Ex. 20:14). David also knew that the palace servants saw and heard everything that went on and reported it to others, so there wasn't much chance he could escape detection. The fact that he was showing interest in his neighbor's wife was probably already public knowledge. But even if nobody but the messenger knew it, the Lord God knew it and didn't approve of what David was doing. God gave David time to come to his senses and seek forgiveness, but he only hardened his heart and continued to pretend that all was well.

2. The committing (2 Sam. 11:4)

One of the puzzles in this event is the willingness of Bathsheba to go with the messengers and submit to David's desires. The Hebrew word translated "took" (laqah) can mean simply "to get, receive, or acquire" or it can be translated "lay hold of, seize, or take away." However, there seems to be no evidence of force or violence in the text and the reader assumes that Bathsheba cooperated with the messengers. But why?

Did Bathsheba even know why David wanted her? If so, didn't

she stop to consider that, having just finished her monthly period (v. 2), she was ripe for conception? Maybe she *wanted* to have a baby by the king! First Kings 1 reveals that Bathsheba was more a tiger than a housecat. "Did the young wife construct the situation?" asks Professor E. M. Blaiklock. "There is more than suspicion that she spread the net into which David so promptly fell."[4] Perhaps she thought David had news from the front about her husband, but it wasn't the king's job to deliver military announcements. Did she miss her husband's love and take her purification bath in public as a deliberate invitation to any man who happened to be watching? If she refused David's requests, would he punish her husband? (That happened anyway!)

No Jewish citizen had to obey a king who himself was disobeying God's law, for the king covenanted with God and the people to submit to the divine law. Did she think that submitting to David would put into her hands a weapon that might help her in the future, especially if her husband were killed in battle? We can ask these questions and many more, but we can't easily answer them. The biblical text doesn't tell us and educated guesses aren't much help.

The sin that David's lust had conceived was now about to be born, a sin that would bring with it sorrow and death. According to Proverbs 6, David was about to be robbed (v. 26), burned (vv. 27-28), disgraced and destroyed (vv. 30-33), just for a few minutes of forbidden pleasure. Hollywood movies, television, and modern fiction use stories about adultery as a means of entertainment, which only shows how bad things have become. Famous people admit they've been unfaithful to their spouses, but it doesn't seem to hurt either their popularity or their incomes. "No-fault divorces" simplify the procedure, but they don't prevent the painful emotional consequences of infidelity. Ministers and other counselors know that it isn't easy for victims to heal and rebuild their lives and homes, yet the media go on teaching people how to break their marriage vows and apparently get away with it.

David and Bathsheba sinned against God, for it is God who

established marriage and wrote the rules that govern it. So serious was adultery in the nation of Israel that both the adulterer and the adulteress were taken out and stoned to death (Lev. 20:10; Deut. 22:22-24; John 8:1-6). God takes seriously the marriage vows brides and grooms make, even if they don't (Mal. 2:14; Heb. 13:4).

3. The covering (2 Sam. 11:5-27)

"And the woman conceived, and sent and told David, and said, I am with child" (v. 5 KJV). These are the only recorded words of Bathsheba in the entire episode, but they were the words David didn't want to hear. You can paraphrase her brief message, "The next step is yours." Being the tactician that he was, David immediately devised a plan to cover up his sin. He called Uriah home from the battlefield, hoping that his brave soldier would go home and spend time with his wife. In fact, David ordered him to go home (v. 8), but the soldier disobeyed and stayed with the king's servants that night. David even sent food from his own table so Uriah and his wife could enjoy a feast, but Uriah never took it home. We wonder if Uriah had heard something that made him suspicious. Palace servants are notorious gossips.

David had to think up another scheme, and his next expedient was to have a second interview with Uriah the next day, during which the king chided him for not going home. A true soldier, Uriah gently rebuked the king for suggesting that one of his own soldiers put personal pleasure ahead of duty, especially when their fellow soldiers were out on the battlefield. Even the ark of God was in a tent, so why should Uriah enjoy his home and wife? First Samuel 21:5 suggests that David's soldiers abstained from intercourse while fulfilling their military duties (a regulation based on Lev. 15:16-18); so Uriah must have been surprised when his commander suggested such a thing.

David's third expedient was to invite Uriah to have a meal with him before he returned to the battle. During the meal, David passed the cup so frequently that Uriah became drunk. But Uriah drunk proved to be a better man than David sober, for he once again refused to go home. Uriah was a soldier at heart, and even when alcohol tore down his defenses, he remained faithful to his calling. There was but one expedient left: Uriah had to die. If David couldn't entice Uriah to go home, he would have to get him out of the way so he could marry Uriah's widow, and the sooner they married, the better the scheme would work. David was breaking the Ten Commandments one by one. He coveted his neighbor's wife and committed adultery with her, and now he would bear false witness against his neighbor and order him to be killed. David thought he was deceiving everybody, but he was deceiving only himself. He thought he could escape guilt when all the while he was adding to his guilt, and he could not escape God's judgment. "He who covers his sins will not prosper" (Prov. 28:13 NKJV).

Joab had Rabbah under siege and ordered his men not to go too near the wall lest they be shot at and killed. Occasionally some Ammonite soldiers would come out the city gate and try to entice the Jewish soldiers to come closer and attack them, but Joab's orders were obeyed. Shrewd Joab may have read between the lines of David's letter and deduced that the only thing Uriah had that David could want would be Uriah's beautiful wife, so he cooperated with the plan. After all, knowing David's scheme would be another weapon Joab could use for his own protection someday. Besides, Joab had already killed Asahel, Abner (2 Sam. 2:17-24; 3:27ff), and would one day murder Amasa (20:6-10), so he understood these things. Joab knew he couldn't send Uriah up to the walls alone or it would look suspicious, so several of "the king's servants" (v. 24) died with him just so David could cover his sins. "The king's servants" may refer to David's bodyguard, the best of the Israelite troops (8:18).

Bathsheba's expressions of grief for her dead warrior husband were undoubtedly sincere, but they were mitigated by the knowledge that she would soon be living in the palace. People probably raised their eyebrows when she married so quickly after the funeral, and married the king at that, but when some six months later she delivered a baby boy, eyebrows went up again. Second

Samuel 3:1-5 suggests Bathsheba as the seventh wife of David, but when you add Michal, who was childless, Bathsheba becomes the eighth. In Scripture, the number eight is often the sign of a new beginning, and with the birth of Solomon to David and Bathsheba, this hope was fulfilled.

However, David had unfinished business to take care of because the Lord was displeased with all he had done.

4. The confessing (2 Sam. 12:1-14)

Nathan had the privilege of delivering the message about God's covenant with David and his descendants (2 Sam. 7), but now the prophet had to perform spiritual surgery and confront the king about his sins. David had been covering his sins for at least six months, and Bathsheba's baby was about to be born. It wasn't an easy task the Lord had given Nathan, but it's obvious that he prepared carefully for his encounter with the guilty king.

The trial (vv. 1-6). In telling a story about the crime of another, Nathan prepared David for dealing with his own sins, and it's possible that David thought Nathan was presenting him with an actual case from the local court. Nathan was catching David off-guard and could study the king's response and better know what to do next. Since David had been a shepherd himself, he would pay close attention to a story about the theft of an innocent lamb; and as king, he was obligated to see that poor families were given justice.

God directed Nathan to choose his words carefully so that they would remind David of what he had said and done. The prophet said that the ewe lamb "did eat of his [the poor man's] own meat, and drank of his own cup, and lay in his bosom" (v. 3 KJV). This should have reminded David of Uriah's speech in 11:11: "Shall I then go to my house to eat and drink, and to lie with my wife?" (NKJV). But it wasn't until Nathan told about the rich man stealing and killing the lamb that David showed any response, and then he was angry at another man's sins! (See 1 Sam. 25:13, 22, 33 for another example of David's anger.) David didn't seem to realize that he was the rich man, Uriah was the poor man, and Bathsheba was the ewe lamb he had stolen. The "traveler" whom the rich man fed represents the temptation and lust that visited David on the roof and then controlled him. If we open the door, sin comes in as a guest but soon becomes the master. (See Gen. 4:6-7.)

David passed judgment on the rich man without realizing he was passing judgment on himself. Of all blindness, the worst kind is that which makes us blind to ourselves. "Many men seem perfect strangers to their own character," said Joseph Butler, and David was among them.[5] How easy it is to be convicted about other people's sins (Matt. 7:1-3)! Stealing and killing a domestic animal wasn't a capital offense in Israel, but David was so angry he exaggerated both the crime and the punishment. Until now, he had been minimizing the consequences and doing nothing, when actually what he did to Uriah *was* worthy of death. Both David and Bathsheba should have been stoned to death (Lev. 20:10; Deut. 22:22-24; John 8:1-6). Knowing the law, David realized that four sheep had to be given to repay the owner whose ewe lamb had been stolen (Ex. 22:1).

The verdict (vv. 7-9). The prophet realized that though David was very angry, he was also unguarded and ready for the sword of the Spirit to pierce his heart (Heb. 4:12; Eph. 6:17). With one quick thrust, Nathan said, "You are the man!" (v. 7 NKJV) and proceeded to hold up the mirror that revealed how dirty the king really was. Nathan explained to David why he stole Uriah's little ewe lamb. First, the king forgot the goodness of the Lord who had given him everything he had *and would have given him more* (v. 7-8). Second, David had despised God's commandment and acted as though he had the privilege of sinning (v. 9). By coveting, committing adultery, bearing false witness, and killing, David had broken four of the Ten Commandments, *and he thought he could get away with it!* It was bad enough that David arranged to have Uriah killed, but he used the sword of the enemy to do it!

The sentence (vv. 10-12). David's adultery with Bathsheba was a sin of passion, a sin of the moment that overtook him, but his sin of having Uriah killed was a premeditated crime that was deliberate and disgraceful. This may be why 1 Kings 15:5 emphasizes "the matter of Uriah the Hittite" and says nothing about Bathsheba. But the Lord judged both sins and David paid dearly for his lust and deceit. God repaid David "in kind" (Deut. 19:21; Ex. 21:23-25; Lev. 24:20), a spiritual principle that David expressed in his "victory psalm" after Saul died (Ps. 18:25-27).

The sword did not depart from the king's household, and his wives were taken and violated just as he had taken Bathsheba. Indeed, David did pay fourfold, for Bathsheba's baby died, and his sons Amnon, Absalom, and Adonijah were slain (13:29; 18:14-15; 1 Kings 2:25). David's beautiful daughter Tamar was raped by her half brother (chap. 13), and David's concubines were humiliated publicly by Absalom when he captured the kingdom (16:22). For the rest of David's lifetime, he experienced one tragedy after another, either in his family or in the kingdom. What a price he paid for those few minutes of passion with his neighbor's wife!

The punishments God assigned to David were already stated in the covenant God had with Israel and which the king was expected to obey (Lev. 26; Deut. 27–30). If the nation rebelled against God, He would slay their sons in battle (Lev. 26:17; Deut. 28:25-26), take away their children (Lev. 26:22; Deut. 28:18), give their wives to others (Deut. 28:30), and even take Israel out of its land into foreign exile (Deut. 28:63-68). Because of Absalom's rebellion, David was forced to flee Jerusalem and live in the wilderness. But the covenant also included a section on repentance and pardon (Deut. 30; Lev. 26:40ff), and David took it seriously.

The pardon (vv. 13-14). The condemned prisoner knew that the verdict was true and the sentence was just, so without any argument, he confessed: "I have sinned against the Lord" (v. 13).[6] Nathan assured David that the Lord had put away his sin. "If we confess our sins, He is faithful and just to forgive us our sins, and to cleanse us from all unrighteousness" (1 John 1:9 NKJV). "If You, Lord, should mark iniquities, O Lord, who could stand? But there is forgiveness with You, that You may be feared" (Ps. 130:3-4 NKJV).

No wonder David later wrote that the Lord "forgives all your iniquities . . . [and] redeems your life from destruction. . . . As far as the east is from the west, so far has He removed our transgressions from us" (Ps. 103:3-4, 12 NKJV).

But there was a "however" in Nathan's reply, for though God in His grace had forgiven David's sins, God in His government had to permit David to experience the consequences of those sins, beginning with the death of Bathsheba's baby. All during David's months of silence, he had suffered intensely, as you can detect when you read his two prayers of confession (Pss. 32 and 51). Psalm 32 pictures a sick old man instead of a virile warrior, and Psalm 51 describes a believer who had lost almost everything—his purity, joy, witness, wisdom, and peace—a man who was afraid God would take the Holy Spirit from him as He had done to Saul. David went through intense emotional and physical pain, but he left behind two prayers that are precious to all believers who have sinned.

Because of Christ's finished work on the cross, God is able to save lost sinners and forgive disobedient saints, and the sooner the lost and the disobedient turn to the Lord and repent, the better off they will be. David wrote, "I said, 'I will confess my transgressions to the Lord,' and You forgave the iniquity of my sin. For this cause everyone who is godly shall pray to You in a time when You may be found" (Ps. 32:5-6 NKJV). "Seek the Lord while He may be found, call upon Him while He is near" (Isa. 55:6 NKJV).

5. The chastening (2 Sam. 12:15-23)

Chastening is not punishment meted out by an angry judge who wants to uphold the law; rather, it's difficulty permitted by a loving Father who wants His children to submit to His will and develop godly character. Chastening is an expression of God's love (Prov. 3:11-12), and the Greek word used in Hebrews 12:5-13 means "child training, instruction, discipline." Greek boys were taken to the gymnasium early in life and taught to run, wrestle, box, swim, and throw, exercises that were assigned so the boys would develop "a sound mind in a sound body." In the

Christian life, chastening isn't always God's response to our disobedience; sometimes He's preparing us for challenges yet to
come, like a coach preparing athletes for the Olympics. If there
were no painful consequences to sin or subsequent chastening
from the hand of God, what kind of a daring and irresponsible
world would we be living in?

Bathsheba delivered the son that Nathan had predicted would
die, but David still fasted and prayed and asked God for healing
for the child. The Lord didn't interrupt David's prayers and tell
him to stop interceding; after all the sins David had committed,
it didn't hurt him to spend the day in prayer. During those
months of silence and separation from God, David had a lot to
catch up on! The baby lived only a week and the parents weren't
able to circumcise and name their son on the eighth day. Their
son Solomon ended up with two names (vv. 24-25), but this son
didn't even have one.

Why would a loving and just God not answer a grieving and
repentant father's prayers and heal the child?[7] After all, it wasn't
the baby's fault that his father and mother had sinned against the
Lord. For that matter, why did God allow Uriah and some fellow
soldiers to die at Rabbah just so David could marry Bathsheba?
Keep asking similar questions and you will end up with the ultimate question, "Why does a loving God permit evil in the
world?" Eventually David looked back and saw this painful experience as God's "goodness and mercy" (Ps. 23:6) both to him and
to the baby. "Shall not the Judge of all the earth do right?" asked
Abraham (Gen. 18:25 NKJV). When he heard the bad news of
God's judgment on his family, even backslidden Eli confessed, "It
is the Lord. Let Him do what seems good to Him" (1 Sam. 3:18
NKJV). There are no easy answers to settle our minds, but there
are plenty of dependable promises to heal our hearts, and faith is
nurtured on promises, not explanations.

This much is sure: David's week of fasting and prayer for the
baby showed his faith in the Lord and his love for Bathsheba and
her little son. Very few Eastern monarchs would have shed a tear
or expressed a sentence of sorrow if a baby died who had been

born to one of the harem "wives." In spite of his many sins, David was still a tender shepherd and a man after God's own heart; he had not been "hardened by the deceitfulness of sin" (Heb. 3:13). He washed himself, changed his apparel, worshiped the Lord, and returned to life with its disappointments and duties. In Scripture, washing oneself and changing clothes symbolizes making a new beginning (Gen. 35:1-2; 41:14; 45:22; Ex. 19:10; Lev. 14:8-9; Jer. 52:33; Rev. 3:18). No matter how long or how much the Lord chastens us, "He will not always strive with us, nor will He keep his anger forever" (Ps. 103:9 NKJV). Because of God's grace and mercy, we can always make a new beginning.

David's words in verse 13 have brought great comfort to people who have experienced the death of a little one, but not every Old Testament student agrees that the king's words are a revelation from God. Perhaps he was just saying, "My son can't come back from the grave or the world of departed spirits, but one day I shall go there to him." But what kind of comfort does it bring us to know that everybody eventually dies? "He shall not return to me" states that David believed that his dead son would neither be reincarnated nor would he be resurrected before the Lord's time. It also affirms that David expected to see and recognize his son in the future life. Where was David eventually going? "I will dwell in the house of the Lord forever" (Ps. 23:6 NKJV; see also 11:7; 16:11; 17:15).[8]

6. The comforting (2 Sam. 12:24-25)

No matter how devastated the chastening hand of our loving Father makes us feel, there is comfort available from the Lord (see Isa. 40:1-2, 9-11, 28-31). Before her son died, God called Bathsheba "Uriah's wife" (v. 15), possibly because that's who she was when the boy was conceived; but in verse 24, she is David's wife, which suggests that, like David, she is also making a new beginning. What an evidence of God's grace that "the wife of Uriah" is mentioned in the genealogy of Messiah (Matt. 1:6), along with Tamar (v. 3; Gen. 38) and Rahab and Ruth (v. 5; Josh. 2 and 6:22-25; Ruth 1, 4; Deut. 23:3).

At least nine months are compressed into verses 24 and 25, nine months of God's grace and tender mercy. It was God who caused the conception to occur and who saw to it that the baby would have the "genetic structure" that he would need to accomplish God's will (Ps. 139:13-16). In a very special way, "the Lord loved him" and even gave Solomon ("peaceable") a special name, "Jedidiah—loved by the Lord." Since "David" means "beloved," father and son were bound together by similar names. God had told David that this son would be born and that he would build the temple (7:12-13; 1 Chron. 22:6-10), and He kept His promise. Every time David and Bathsheba looked at Solomon, his very presence reminded them that God had forgiven their past and guaranteed their plans for the future.

7. The conquering (2 Sam. 12:26-31; 1 Chron. 20:1-3)

But there was still kingdom work for David to do, including helping Joab finish the siege of Rabbah (10:14; 11:1; 12:26-31). Little by little, the Israelite army had taken over the city, first the area where the royal palace stood (v. 26), and then the section that controlled the water supply (v. 27). Joab was now ready for that final assault that would bring the siege to an end, but he wanted the king to be there to lead the army. Whatever his faults, Joab at least wanted to bring honor to his king. David went to Rabbah and led the troops in the final foray that brought the city to its knees.

No king could wear a crown very long that weighed from fifty to seventy-five pounds, so David's "coronation" was a brief but official act of state, claiming Ammon as his territory. (The imperial state crown used by the kings and queens of England weighs less than three pounds, and monarchs have found wearing it a bit of a burden!) The crown was very valuable, so David took it along with the abundant spoil he found in the city. Most of this wealth probably went into the Lord's treasury and was used in the building of the temple.

David put some of his prisoners of war to work with saws, picks and axes, and others to making bricks. God in His grace gave

David this victory even though he had been a rebellious man. He and his army then returned to Jerusalem where he would experience further chastening, this time from adult members of his own family. He had forced the Ammonites to drop their swords, but now the sword would be drawn in his own family.

SIX

David's Unruly Sons

We have seen in the first ten chapters of 2 Samuel how God empowered David to defeat Israel's enemies and establish and expand the kingdom. Then David committed the sins of adultery, murder, and deception (chap. 11-12), and the rest of the book describes David wrestling with problems caused by his own children. His days are dark and disappointing, but he still depends on the Lord, and the Lord enables him to overcome and prepare the nations for the reign of his son Solomon. What life does to us depends on what life finds in us, and in David was a muscular faith in the living God.

Absalom is the chief actor in this part of the drama, for it was Absalom who helped to turn the drama into a tragedy.[1] The three heirs to David's throne were Amnon, David's firstborn, Absalom, his third son,[2] and Adonijah, who was born fourth (1 Chron. 3:1-2). God had warned David that the sword would not depart from his own household (12:10), and Absalom (which means "peaceful") was the first to take up that sword. David's judgment against the rich man in Nathan's story was, "He shall restore the lamb fourfold" (12:6), and that judgment fell upon David's own head. Bathsheba's baby died; Absalom killed Amnon for raping Tamar;

Joab killed Absalom during the battle of Mount Ephraim; and Adonijah was slain for trying to usurp the throne from Solomon (1 Kings 2:12-25).

David was reigning over Israel, but sin and death were reigning within his own family (Rom. 5:14, 17, 21). God had forgiven David's sins (12:13), but David was discovering that the consequences of *forgiven* sin are very painful. God had blessed David with many sons (1 Chron. 28:5), but now the Lord would turn some of those blessings into curses (Mal. 2:1-2). "Your own wickedness will correct you, and your backslidings will rebuke you" (Jer. 2:19 NKJV). The events in chapters 13 and 14 unfold like a tragic symphony in five movements: from love to lust (13:1-14), from lust to hatred (13:15-22), from hatred to murder (13:23-36), from murder to exile (13:37-39), and from exile to reconciliation (14:1-23).

1. From love to lust (2 Sam. 13:1-14)
Absalom is mentioned first because chapters 13-19 focus on the "Absalom story," and Tamar was Absalom's full sister. Both Tamar and Absalom were noted for their physical beauty (13:1; 14:25). Their mother was Maacah, a princess from the royal house of Talmai in Geshur, a small Aramean kingdom near what we know as the Sea of Galilee. David had no doubt taken Maacah as his wife in order to establish a peace treaty with her father. The fact that Absalom had royal blood in his veins from both his father and his mother may have spurred him on in his egotistical quest for the kingdom.

Amnon was the oldest of David's sons and the apparent heir to the throne, so perhaps he felt he had privileges that the other sons didn't have. It was evil for him to nurture an abnormal love for his half sister and he should have stopped feeding that appetite the moment it started (Matt. 5:27-30). The sin was not only unnatural, but it violated the standard of sexual purity established by God's law (Lev. 18:9-11; 20:17; Deut. 27:22). However, he became so infatuated with Tamar that he really thought he loved her and became ill thinking about it. The virgin princesses were kept secluded in their own quarters, apart even from their male relatives, and Amnon's imagination worked overtime as he thought about her.

Jonadab was Amnon's cousin, the son of David's brother Shammah, here called Shimeah (1 Sam. 16:9), and he was a very crafty man, probably a minor official in the palace. He will show up again in 14:32 after Amnon has been killed by Absalom's servants. Anybody in our lives who makes it easy for us to sin is certainly not much of a friend; in fact, by following Jonadab's advice, Amnon ended up becoming a rapist, committing incest, and getting killed.

Amnon must have begun to recover from his "love sickness" because he had to pretend to be ill when David came to visit him. Perhaps Amnon was thinking, "If my father committed adultery and murder and got away with it, surely I can get away with rape." Such is the destructive power of a bad example. "If the godly compromise with the wicked, it is like polluting a fountain or muddying a spring" (Prov. 25:26 NLT). David's family was now polluted and the consequences would be calamitous. David was known for his wisdom and keen insight (14:17, 20), but after the "Bathsheba affair," he seems to have lost ground. By ordering Tamar to obey her half brother's wishes, he sent her into pain and humiliation; and when two years later David allowed Amnon to attend Absalom's feast, he sent his firstborn to his death. David the deceiver was himself deceived!

Tamar baked the special cakes for Amnon, who asked everyone to leave so he could enjoy the meal with his sister, and then he forcibly violated her. What he thought was love was really only lust, a passion that so controlled him that he became like an animal. Of course she resisted him as long as she could. Her refusal to cooperate was based on the law of God and the responsibility of the nation of Israel to be different from their pagan neighbors (v. 12). David's sin had given occasion to the enemy to blaspheme God (12:14). Her use of the words "folly" and "fool" (vv. 12-13 KJV) remind us of Genesis 34 and Judges 19–20, two other despicable rape scenes in Scripture. (See Gen. 34:7;

Jud. 19:23-24; 20:6, 10.) Tamar tried to stall for time by suggesting that he ask the king for permission to marry her (v. 13), even though she knew that such a marriage was prohibited by the Law of Moses (Lev. 18:9-11; 20:17; Deut. 27:22).[3]

2. From lust to hatred (2 Sam. 13:15-22)

Amon thought he loved Tamar. First he was distressed over her (vv. 1-2), and then he became ill longing for her (v. 2) even to the point of looking haggard (v. 4). But after he committed the shameful act, he hated Tamar vehemently and wanted to get rid of her! True love would never violate another person's body just to satisfy selfish appetites, nor would true love try to persuade someone to disobey the law of God. In his sensual cravings, Amnon confused lust with love and didn't realize that there is a fine line between selfish love (lust) and hatred. Before he sinned, he wanted Tamar all to himself; but after he sinned, he couldn't get rid of her fast enough.

Sexual sins usually produce that kind of emotional damage. When you treat other people like things to be used, you end up throwing them aside like broken toys or old clothes. The word "woman" is not in the Hebrew text of verse 17, so Amnon was saying, "Throw this thing out!" This explains why Tamar accused Amnon of being even more cruel by casting her aside than by raping her. Having lost her virginity, Tamar was not a good prospect for marriage, and she could no longer reside in the apartments with the virgins. Where would she go? Who would take her in? Who would even want her? How could she prove that Amnon was the aggressor and that she hadn't seduced him?

She went to the apartment of her brother Absalom, because in a polygamous society, it was the responsibility of a full brother to protect the honor of a full sister.[4] When Absalom saw her tears, her torn garment, and the ashes on her head, he realized that she was in great pain and humiliation, and he deduced that Amnon had violated her. His question "Has that Amnon[5] your brother, been with you?" (v. 20 NIV) reveals this, for the phrase "been with you" was a euphemism for "gone to bed with you." Palace gossips don't miss much, so it's probable that Absalom heard of Amnon's "illness" and Tamar's intended visit to his apartment. But if Absalom was so concerned about his sister, why didn't he warn her to stay away from Amnon? The king had ordered Tamar to visit her half brother, and Absalom's words couldn't change the king's command. About all Absalom could do was caution her not to be left alone with him.

Tamar may have said that she was going to the king to tell him what happened, but her brother suggested that she wait. Why? Because Absalom's cunning brain was already at work on a scheme that would accomplish three purposes: avenge Tamar, get rid of Amnon, and put himself next in line for the throne! His statement "He is your brother" (v. 20) means, "If it were any other man, I would avenge you immediately; but since it's your brother, I'll have to be patient and wait for an opportunity." Absalom was trying to avoid a public scandal that would grieve the family and hurt his own plans to seize the throne.

King David did hear about the tragedy and became very angry, but what could he say? The memory of his own sins shut his mouth, and how could he punish his firstborn son and the heir to his throne? According to the law, if a man raped a virgin not engaged to be married, he had to pay her father a fine and marry her, and he could never divorce her (Deut. 22:28-29). However, the law also prohibited the marriage of half brothers and half sisters, so marriage was out of the question (Lev. 18:9). David had committed two capital crimes—adultery and murder—and God had not applied the law to him.

So, neither David nor Absalom said anything to Amnon about his wicked deed. In fact, Absalom never spoke to him at all ("neither good nor bad") but simply waited for the right time to kill Amnon and avenge his sister. However, Amnon's friend Jonadab knew that Absalom wanted to kill Amnon, for he said, ". . . by the intent of Absalom this has been determined since the day that he violated his sister Tamar" (13:32 NASB). If Jonadab figured out what was going on, perhaps others suspected something also. Amnon's lust had turned to hatred, but now it was

Absalom who was nurturing hatred in his heart, and that hatred would give birth to murder (Matt. 5:21-22). Then, with Amnon out of the way, Absalom could become king.[6]

3. From hatred to murder (2 Sam. 13:23-36)

The French author Emile Gaboriau wrote, "Revenge is a luscious fruit which you must leave to ripen." For two years Absalom waited to avenge the rape of his sister, but when the time came, he was ready to act. Thanks to the generosity of their father, the princes not only held government offices but they also owned lands, flocks, and herds. Absalom had his land and flocks at Baal Hazor, about fourteen miles north of Jerusalem. It was customary in Israel to arrange great feasts at sheep-shearing time and invite members of the family as well as friends to share the festive occasion.

Absalom asked his father to come to the feast and bring his officials with him, but David declined, explaining that so many guests would be an unnecessary financial burden to his son. Absalom was hoping for that kind of response because he didn't want David and his guards present when Amnon was murdered. Then he asked if David would permit his successor Amnon to attend the feast, a request that made David feel apprehensive. But David knew that the crown prince often took his place at public functions that demanded royal presence, so why couldn't he represent the throne at Absalom's feast? Furthermore, two years had passed since Amnon violated Tamar and Absalom hadn't done anything against him. To guarantee some kind of safety for Amnon, David went the extra mile and permitted all the adult king's sons to attend the feast, assuming that Absalom wouldn't dare attack Amnon with so many of his family members present.

But during those two years, Absalom had perfected his plan and made arrangements for escape. His father David had arranged for the murder of Uriah the Hittite and had survived, so why shouldn't his son Absalom survive? Like his father, Absalom used other hands to do the deed, and at a time when the victim least expected it. David had made Uriah drunk but had failed to achieve his purpose, while Absalom made his brother drunk and accomplished what he had set out to do. Absalom followed his father's evil example and committed premeditated murder.

When Absalom gave the command and his servants killed Amnon, the princes at the feast fled for their lives, no doubt convinced that Absalom was planning to wipe out the royal family and take the throne. The young men mounted their mules, which were considered a "royal animal" (18:9; 1 Kings 1:33, 38, 44), and they hastened back to Jerusalem as fast as the animals could move. But Absalom also fled (vv. 34, 37) and probably his servants with him.

In verses 30-36, which are a parenthesis, we move from Baal Hazor to Jerusalem and see the escaping princes from David's point of view. Before the guards on the wall could clearly observe the men riding furiously toward Jerusalem and recognize them as the king's sons, a messenger arrived from Absalom's house announcing that all the king's sons had been slain! (Bad news travels fast and often is exaggerated.) David tore his garments and fell to the ground in grief (see 12:16), no doubt blaming himself for allowing his sons to attend Absalom's feast. David's nephew Jonadab, who knew more than he admitted,[7] gave the true account that only Amnon had been killed; but even this was a terrible blow to David, for Amnon was his firstborn and heir to the throne. The fleeing princes arrived safely and everyone joined in expressing grief because Amnon was dead and Absalom was the murderer.

The problem with revenge is that it doesn't really solve any problems and eventually turns around and hurts the perpetrator. "In taking revenge," wrote Francis Bacon, "a man is but even with his enemy, but in passing it over, he is superior."[8] No one was treated more unjustly and inhumanely than Jesus Christ at His trial and crucifixion, yet He refused to retaliate; and He is our example (1 Peter 2:18-25). The old slogan "Don't get mad—get even" may satisfy some people, but it can never be pleasing to the Lord. The Christian way is the way of forgiveness and faith, trusting the Lord to work everything out for our good and His glory (1 Peter 4:12-19).

4. From murder to exile (2 Samuel 13:37-39)

Twice we're told that Absalom fled (vv. 34, 37), and he probably did it during the confusion that ensued when the king's sons fled. Only Absalom and his guilty servants knew what was going to happen at the feast, so everybody else was caught unawares. They were all witnesses of the "murder most foul" and could easily testify that Absalom was guilty.

Absalom fled eighty miles northeast to the home of his maternal grandparents in Geshur, where his grandfather Talmai was king (3:3). No doubt this safe haven had been arranged beforehand, and it's likely that Talmai would have enjoyed seeing his grandson crowned king of Israel. Back in Jerusalem, David mourned over his firstborn son Amnon, but in Geshur, the exiled son was no doubt plotting how he could take the kingdom away from his father. Normal grief heals in its time, and after three years, David was comforted concerning the death of the crown prince.

The statement "And the soul of king David longed to go forth unto Absalom" (v. 39 KJV) has been given at least two interpretations. It means either that David wanted very much to see his son again, which is understandable, or that David planned to go after Absalom and deal with him, but his anger gradually quieted down. I prefer the second interpretation. If David had really wanted Absalom back home, he could have accomplished it very easily, since Joab was for it (14:22) and David's in-laws in Geshur would have cooperated. However, when Absalom did come home, David kept him at a distance for two years (14:28)! If the king was anxious to see his son again, he went about it in a peculiar way. It appears that a struggle was going on in David's heart: he knew that his son deserved punishment, but David was known for being lenient with his sons (1 Kings 1:6). David initially planned to deal severely with Absalom but decided against it as his attitude changed. As explained in chapter 14, David compromised by finally bringing Absalom home, but he punished him by delaying full reconciliation. It was five years before father and son saw each other face-to-face (13:38; 14:28).

5. From exile to reconciliation (2 Sam. 14:1-33)

Joab knew his king very well and recognized the signs of David's yearning for his exiled son. As head of the army, Joab was concerned that Israel have a crown prince ready to reign just in case something happened to David, who was now close to sixty. But Absalom couldn't come home unless David gave permission, and the king wouldn't give permission until he was convinced it was the right thing to do. It was the king's duty to uphold the law, and Absalom was guilty of plotting the murder of his half brother Amnon.[9]

David loved his son and undoubtedly was convicted about the way he had pampered him, but how could he get out of this dilemma? Joab provided the solution to the problem.

Joab reasons with the king (vv. 1-20). Just as Nathan had confronted David the sinner by telling him a story (12:1-7), so Joab confronted David the father and king by putting a fabricated account of a family problem into the mouth of a woman who was both wise and a very good actress. She came to the king dressed in mourning and told him about her family troubles. Her two sons had an argument in the field and the one killed the other. (This sounds like Cain and Abel, Gen. 4:8-16.) The other relatives wanted to slay the guilty son and avenge his brother's blood (Num. 35:6ff; Deut. 19:1-14), but she opposed them. Killing her only son would put an end to her family and "quench her coal" (v. 7). According to the law, the surviving son was guilty and should be slain (Ex. 21:12; Lev. 24:17), but she wanted the king to pardon her surviving son.

Nathan's story about the ewe lamb touched the heart of David the shepherd, and this story about a warring family moved the heart of David the father. His first response was to assure her he would "take up the case" (v. 8), but that wasn't good enough for her. Sometimes the wheels of government turn slowly, and her case was a matter of life and death. When she said she would assume the guilt of whatever decision he made, David promised to protect her if anybody approached her about the matter (vv. 9-10). But the woman still wasn't satisfied, so she asked the king to take an oath to assure her that her son would not be slain, and David agreed (v. 11). Taking an oath in the Lord's name was binding and could not be ignored.

The woman now had David in a corner (vv. 12-17). If he had agreed to protect a guilty son whom he did not know, how much more was he obligated to protect his own son whom he loved! She had come to him with a matter involving the future of one small family, but the matter concerning Absalom concerned the future of an entire nation. The king didn't want to see her only son and heir destroyed, but he was willing for the crown prince to be left in exile. He forgave the murderer of her son, so could he not forgive the man who plotted the murder of Amnon? How much longer will the king wait before he sends for his son? After all, life is brief, and when life ends, it's like water spilled into the earth and can't be recovered. Slaying the murderer can't bring back the victim, so why not give him another chance?

God is no respecter of persons, and His law is true, but even God devises ways to show mercy and forgive offenders (v. 14). He punishes sin, to be sure, but He also seeks for ways to reconcile sinners with Himself. (She may have had in mind Ex. 32:30-35 and 34:6-9.) Had He not forgiven David's sins? The woman confessed that she was afraid that her family would slay her son and rob her of the inheritance God had given them.

It was a stirring speech and David took it to heart. But being a wise man, he realized that the full import of the woman's plea went far beyond the boundaries of her family and property. David had insight enough to know that she was speaking about the king, Absalom, and the future of the nation of Israel, God's inheritance. At this point he also must have understood that the entire story was pure fiction and that somebody else was behind all that the so-called widow had spoken. Then the truth came out that indeed it was Joab who had plotted the whole thing, but his motive was a noble one: "Your servant Joab did this to change the present situation" (v. 20 NIV).

Joab gives thanks to the king (vv. 21-27). No doubt it was Joab who brought the woman to have this audience with the king, and he probably remained in the room and heard all that the woman and the king said to each other. David had sworn to protect the woman and her son, so the king could do nothing but allow Absalom to come home; and he ordered Joab to go to Geshur and bring the exile back to Jerusalem. Joab's words in verse 22 suggest strongly that he had discussed the subject with David on more than one occasion, and he was overjoyed that the matter was now settled. Geshur was about eighty miles from Jerusalem, and Joab would waste no time making the journey; so Absalom could have been back home a week or ten days later.

However, there were restrictions placed on the crown prince. He had to remain on his own land, which almost amounted to house arrest, and he wasn't allowed to go to the palace and see his father. Perhaps David was testing his son to see if he could be trusted, or David may have thought that these restrictions would assure the people that the king wasn't pampering his difficult son. However, these limitations didn't hinder the expansion of Absalom's popularity, for the people loved and praised him. The fact that he had plotted the murder of his half brother and had proved his guilt by running away meant very little to the people, for people must have their idols, and what better idol than a young handsome prince? Lack of character was unimportant; what really mattered was status, wealth, and good looks.[10] In contemporary language, Absalom was a he-man, someone with "machismo," and the people envied and admired him. Times have not changed.

Whatever Absalom may have had, one thing he didn't have was a large number of sons to carry on his "famous" name. The three sons mentioned in verse 27 must have died very young, because 18:18 informs us that Absalom had no sons living at that time. We aren't surprised that he named his daughter after his sister Tamar. Always the egotist, Absalom erected a pillar to remind everybody of his greatness.

Joab brings Absalom to the king (vv. 28-33). A deceptive "wise woman" could see the king's face, but the king's own son was banished from his presence. Absalom put up with this arrange-

ment for two years, trusting that Joab would bring about reconciliation between himself and his father, but Joab did nothing.
Absalom knew that being banished from the king's presence
meant he wasn't expected to be heir to the throne, and more
than anything else, Absalom wanted to be king of Israel. A
shrewd man like Joab must have realized that Absalom had
designs on the throne and that the prince's growing popularity
could provide him the support he needed to take over the kingdom. Knowing how volatile the situation was, the discerning
general stayed away from Absalom lest he give the impression he
was being controlled by the egotistical prince.

After two years of waiting, during which he had summoned
Joab twice and been ignored, Absalom decided that drastic
action was necessary. He commanded his servants to set fire to
his neighbor's barley crop, and his neighbor happened to be
Joab.[11] This got the general's attention, for the law required that
an arsonist repay the owner of a field whose crop he had
destroyed (Ex. 22:6). People knew about the fire, so Joab could
visit Absalom without fear of being misunderstood.

Absalom presented Joab with two alternatives: either take him
to the king and let him receive his son and forgive him, or take
him to court and prove that he was guilty of a capital crime and
deserved to die. Absalom would rather be slain than go on living
in shameful house arrest. Joab was on the horns of a dilemma, for
it was he who had masterminded Absalom's return to Jerusalem.
Joab knew that the people would never permit their favorite
royal personage to be tried and convicted of a crime, but how
could Joab guarantee that the king would be reconciled to his
son? Joab gave Absalom's message to David and David invited his
son to come to see him, and the king received him with a kiss of
reconciliation. Father and son were together after five years of
separation (13:38; 14:28).

There is no record that Absalom was repentant and sought his
father's forgiveness, or that he visited the temple and offered the
required sacrifices. Father and son were together again, but it was
a fragile truce and not a real peace. Absalom still had his hidden

agenda and was determined to seize David's throne. Now that the prince was free, he could be visible in the city and enjoy the adulation of the crowds, while at the same time quietly organizing his sympathizers for the coming rebellion. David was about to lose his throne and crown, his concubines, his trusted adviser Ahithophel, and ultimately his son Absalom. It would be the darkest hour in David's life.

David's Escape to the Wilderness

It's one thing to experience God's power when you're facing giants or fighting armies, and quite something else when you're watching people tear your world apart. God was chastening David, but David knew that God's power could help him in the hour of pain as well as in the hour of conquest. He wrote in one of his exile psalms, "Many are they who say of me, 'There is no help for him in God.' But You, O Lord, are a shield for me, my glory and the One who lifts up my head" (Ps. 3:2-3 NKJV). David recognized that God's loving hand of discipline was upon him, and he admitted that he deserved every blow. But he also believed that God's gracious hand of power was still at work in his life, that the Lord hadn't forsaken him as He forsook Saul. The Lord was still working out His perfect will, and never did David rise to greater heights of faith and submission than when he was forced to leave Jerusalem and hide in the wilderness.

The passage introduces us to three kings.

1. Absalom—Israel's counterfeit king (2 Sam. 15:1-12)

If ever a man was equipped to be a demagogue[1] and lead people astray, that man was Absalom. He was a handsome man whose charm was difficult to resist (14:25-26), and he had royal blood in his veins from both his father and his mother. The fact that he had no character wasn't important to most of the people who, like sheep, would follow anybody who told them what they wanted to hear and gave them what they wanted to have. Newspaper editor H. L. Mencken's definition of a demagogue is rather extreme, but he gets the point across: "One who preaches doctrines he knows to be untrue to men he knows to be idiots." Novelist James Fenimore Cooper expressed it accurately: "One who advances his own interests by affecting a deep devotion to the interests of the people."

Absalom was not only a consummate liar, but he was a patient man who was able to discern just the right hour to act. He waited two years before having Amnon murdered (13:23), and now he waited four years before openly rebelling against his father and seizing the throne (v. 7).[2] When you read the "exile psalms" of David, you get the impression that at this time King David was ill and didn't have his hands on the affairs of the kingdom, thus giving Absalom opportunity to move in and take over.[3] With great skill, the egotistical prince used every device at his disposal to mesmerize the people and win their support. David had won the hearts of the people through sacrifice and service, but Absalom did it the easy way—and the modern way—by manufacturing an image of himself that the people couldn't resist. David was a hero; Absalom was only a celebrity. Alas, many of the people had gotten accustomed to their king and now took him for granted.

Absalom's campaign must have begun shortly after his reconciliation with his father, for now he was free to go wherever he pleased. His first move was to begin riding in a chariot pulled by horses and accompanied by fifty men who were his bodyguard and who announced his presence. The prophet Samuel had predicted this kind of behavior by Israel's kings (1 Sam. 8:11) and Moses had warned against the acquisition of horses (Deut. 17:16). David wrote in Psalm 20:7 (NKJV), "Some trust in chariots, and some in horses; but we will remember the name of the Lord our God."

Since David wasn't available to the people, Absalom met them personally on the road to the city gate when they came early each morning to have their grievances examined and their cases tried. The city gate was the "city hall" of the ancient cities (Ruth 4:1ff; Gen. 23:10; Deut. 22:15; 25:7), and he knew there would be many disgruntled people there wondering why the court system wasn't functioning efficiently. (See 2 Sam. 19:1-8.) Absalom would greet these visitors like old friends and find out where they came from and what their problems were. He agreed with all of them their complaints were right and should be settled in their favor by the king's court. It was gross flattery of the most despicable kind, but the people loved it. Absalom boasted that he would handle kingdom matters better if only he were a judge (v. 4), which was a subtle way of criticizing his father. When people started to bow to him because he was the crown prince, he reached out his hand and stopped them, pulled them to himself and kissed them (v. 5). This reminds us of the hypocritical kisses of Judas when he greeted Jesus in the garden (Matt. 26:47-50; Mark 14:45).

It took only four years for Absalom's magnetism to draw together a large number of devoted followers throughout the whole land. The people Absalom met returned home and told their friends and neighbors that they had spoken personally to the crown prince, and over the four-year period, this kind of endorsement won Absalom many friends. His rapid success at influencing the minds and hearts of a nation warns us that one day a leader will arise who will control the minds of people around the world (Rev. 13:3; 2 Thes. 2). Even the people of Israel will be deceived and sign a covenant with this ruler, and then he will turn on them and seek to destroy them (Dan. 9:26-27). Jesus told the Jewish leaders of His day, "I have come in My Father's name, and you do not receive me; if another comes in his own name, him you will receive" (John 5:43 NKJV).

Absalom had been deceiving his siblings and the Jewish nation for years, and when the right time came, he took a bold step and lied to his father (vv. 7-9). The prince was no longer under house arrest, so there was no need to get permission to leave Jerusalem, but in so doing he achieved several purposes. First, he could tell anybody who asked that he had his father's permission to go to Hebron to fulfill the vow he had made while exiled in Geshur. Second, it allayed any fears that might arise because of Absalom's former feast at which Amnon was killed. Third, it gave credence to his invitation to two hundred key people in David's administration who willingly attended the feast. When the guests saw these two hundred important people in Hebron, they must have been impressed. The fact that this was a feast connected with the fulfilling of a vow gave it the aura of a religious assembly (Deut. 23:21-23), for sacrifices were offered to the Lord. What could go wrong at a feast dedicated to the Lord? Absalom was now using the name of the Lord to hide his sins.[4]

Absalom's masterstroke was to win the support of Ahithophel, David's smartest counselor; and when the guests saw him at the feast, they felt confident that all was well. But Ahithophel did more than attend the celebration; he also joined Absalom in revolting against King David. It was probably Ahithophel who masterminded the entire operation. After all, David had violated Ahithophel's granddaughter Bathsheba and ordered her husband killed. (See 23:34; 1 Chron. 3:5.) This was Ahithophel's great opportunity to avenge himself on David. However, in supporting Absalom, Ahithophel was rejecting Bathsheba's son Solomon, whom God would choose to be the next ruler of Israel. At the same time, Ahithophel was taking steps toward his own death for, like Judas, he rejected the true king and went out and committed suicide. (See 17:23; Pss. 41:9; 55:12-14; Matt. 26:21-25; John 13:18; Acts 1:16.) Ahithophel had deceived David his king and sinned against the Lord, who had chosen David.

Why did Absalom decide to start his insurrection in Hebron? For one thing, it was the former capital of Judah, and perhaps there were people there who resented David's moving the capital to Jerusalem. Absalom was born in Hebron and could claim special kinship with the residents. Hebron was a sacred city to the Jews because it was assigned to the priests and had a connection with Caleb (Josh. 21:8-16). Located about twenty miles south-west of Jerusalem, Hebron was a walled city and the ideal city from which to invade Jerusalem and seize the throne. With two hundred of David's officials "imprisoned" behind Hebron's walls, it would be simple for Absalom to take over the kingdom.

2. David—Israel's true king (2 Sam. 15:13-23)

Absalom and Ahithophel had their trumpeters and messengers ready to act, and at the signal, the word quickly spread through-out the land: "Absalom is king! He reigns from Hebron!" The anonymous messenger who informed David actually helped to save the king's life. However lethargic David may have been before now, he immediately moved into action, because David always did his best during a crisis.

David takes charge (vv. 13-16). His first official order was for his family, officials and special bodyguard to leave Jerusalem imme-diately. If Absalom had the whole nation following him, it would be easy for armies from Judah and the northern tribes to surround Jerusalem and leave no way of escape. David knew that the same Absalom who killed Amnon would also kill his brothers and pos-sibly even his father, so it was imperative that everybody flee. Furthermore, if Absalom had to attack Jerusalem, he would slaughter the inhabitants, and there was no reason for hundreds of innocent people to die. It was just like David to risk his own life and abandon his own throne in order to protect others. The servants pledged their loyalty to the king (v. 16) and so did the his bodyguard (vv. 18-22). The ten concubines David left behind to manage the household would be violated by Absalom (16:20-23), an act that declared he had taken over his father's kingdom.

David mobilizes the forces (vv. 17-22). David and the people with him escaped to the northeast, moving from Jerusalem opposite the direction of Hebron. When they came to the last house in the suburbs of Jerusalem, they rested and David reviewed his troops. These included David's personal bodyguard (the Cherethites and the Pelethites, 8:18; 23:22-23) as well as six hundred Philistines who had followed David from Gath and were under the command of Ittai (1 Sam. 27:3). Ittai assured David that they were completely loyal to the king. This Gentile's testimony of fidelity to David (v. 21) is one of the great confessions of faith and faithfulness found in Scripture and ranks with that of Ruth (1:16) and the Roman centurion (Matt. 8:5-13).[5]

David weeps (v. 23). The key word in this section is "passed over" or "crossed over," used nine times. David and his people crossed the Kidron (v. 23), which in winter flowed powerfully on the east side of Jerusalem and had to be crossed to reach the Mount of Olives. The scene reminds us of our Lord's experience when He went to the garden (John 18:1). At that very hour, Judas, one of His own disciples, was betraying Him and arranging for His arrest. The people wept as they quickly moved along and their king wept with them, though perhaps for a different reason (vv. 23, 30). His own son had betrayed him, along with his friend and confidential adviser, and the foolish people for whom the king had done so much were ignorant of what was going on. David might have prayed as Jesus did on the cross, "Father, forgive them, for they know not what they do" (Luke 23:34).

Was David feeling the weight of guilt as once again Absalom, his beloved son, defied God's will and broke his father's heart? He and his son had been reconciled, but the young man had shown no contrition for his sins nor had he asked forgiveness from his father or from the Lord. "The sword shall not depart from your household" had been the ominous sentence from the mouth of God's prophet, and it was being fulfilled. Bathsheba's baby had died and Amnon had been murdered. David didn't want Absalom to die (18:5), but the young man would be slain by Joab, the third "installment" in David's painful payment (12:6). Adonijah would also die in an aborted attempt to become king (1 Kings 1), and then the debt would be paid.

For the second time in his life, David is forced to flee into the wilderness to save his life. As a young man, he fled the jealous rage of King Saul, and now he was seeking refuge from the hypocritical deceptions of his son Absalom and his former counselor Ahithophel. By leaving Jerusalem, David had spared the city a bloodbath, but now he and his family were in danger, and what was the future of the kingdom and God's covenant with David?

3. Jehovah—Israel's sovereign King (2 Sam. 15:24–16:14)

When you read David's exile psalms, you can't help but see his trust in God and his conviction that no matter how disordered and disturbed everything was, the Lord was still on His throne. No matter how David felt, he knew that the Lord would always keep His covenant and fulfill His promises. Psalm 4 might well have been the song David sang to God that first evening away from home, and Psalm 3 what he prayed the next morning. In Psalms 41 and 55, he poured out his heart to the Lord, and the Lord heard him and answered in His time. Psalms 61, 62, and 63 allow us to look into David's troubled heart as he asks God for guidance and strength. Note that each of these three psalms ends with a strong affirmation of faith in the Lord. We today can have courage and assurance in our own times of difficulty as we see how the Lord responded to David and his great needs.

The Lord acknowledges David's faith (15:24-29). Zadok and Abiathar shared the high priestly duties and had helped to bring the ark to Jerusalem (1 Chron. 15:11ff), so they thought it wise to take the ark to David. Absalom had usurped his father's throne, but the priests would not allow him to have the throne of God. They joined David's camp and brought many of the Levites with them, and Abiathar offered sacrifices (v. 24 NIV) and no doubt called upon God to guide and protect the king.

But David told them to take the ark back to Jerusalem! He didn't want the throne of God treated like a good-luck charm as in the days of Eli when the glory departed from Israel (1 Sam. 4). Absalom and his men were trying to turn David's glory into shame (Ps. 4:2), but God's favor was upon the king and He would restore him to his throne. David had seen God's power and glory in His sanctuary (Ps. 63:2 and he would see it by faith there in the wilderness. But even if God rejected David, the king was prepared to accept Jehovah's sovereign will (v. 26).[6] Eli had made a similar statement (1 Sam. 3:18), but it was resignation, not dedication. In David's case, the king was totally yielding to the Lord and saying, "Not my will but your will be done."

Faith without works is dead, so David assigned the two priests to be his eyes and ears in Jerusalem and to send him all the information that would help him plan his strategy. Zadok's son Ahimaaz and Jonathan the son of Abiathar would be the messengers and bring the information to him. David was a gifted tactician, and when you read 1 Samuel 19–28, you discover that he had an effective spy system that kept him informed of Saul's every move. David would have agreed with the counsel attributed to Oliver Cromwell, "Put your trust in God, my boys, and keep your powder dry." Whatever Absalom might do to the king's officials, he wasn't likely to lay hands on the Lord's priests and Levites, and they could go about their work almost unnoticed. When the two priests and their sons returned to Jerusalem with the ark, Absalom's followers must have interpreted their action as four votes for the new king.

The Lord sees David's tears (15:30). "The Bible was written in tears, and to tears it will yield its best treasures," said A. W. Tozer.[7] David was a strong and courageous man, but he wasn't afraid to weep openly. (Real men *do* weep, including Jesus and Paul.) We read about David's tears in Psalm 6, which might well have been an exile psalm (vv. 6-8), as well as in Psalms 30:5, 39:12, and 56:8. "Depart from me, all you workers of iniquity; for the Lord has heard the voice of my weeping" (Ps. 6:8 NKJV). "The sacrifices of God are a broken spirit, a broken and a contrite heart—these, O God, You will not despise" (Ps. 51:17 NKJV).

David certainly had much to weep over, for his sins had brought sorrow and death to his family. Amnon had been murdered and Tamar violated, and now Absalom—the king's own son—was in the process of usurping the throne of Israel and heading for certain death. David's friend and counselor Ahithophel had turned against him, and the people for whom David had often risked his life were abandoning him to follow an egotistical rebel who was never chosen by God. If ever a man had a right to weep, it was David. Like disobedient children being spanked, it's easy for people to weep when they're being chastened for their sins, and then forget about the pain when the spanking is over. But David's tears went much deeper. He was not only concerned for the welfare of his rebellious son but also for the safety of the nation and the future of Israel's God-given ministry to the world. God's covenant with David (2 Sam. 7) assured him that his throne would last forever, and this is fulfilled in Christ; but the promise also implied that Israel would not be destroyed or **the** lamp of David permanently extinguished (1 Kings 11:36; 15:4; 2 Kings 8:19; 21:7; Ps. 132:17). God would be faithful to keep His covenant, and David knew that his throne was safe in the hands of the Lord.

The Lord answers David's prayer (15:31-37). Another messenger arrived in David's camp and informed the king that Ahithophel had deserted him for Absalom (see v. 12). "Even my own familiar friend in whom I trusted, who ate my bread, has lifted up his heel against me" (Ps. 41:9 NKJV). "For it is not an enemy who reproaches me; then I could bear it. . . . But it was you, a man my equal, my companion and my acquaintance" (Ps. 55:11-14). What do you do when one of your closest confidants betrays you? You do what David did—you pray and you worship. "O Lord, I pray thee, turn the counsel of Ahithophel into foolishness. And it came to pass, that when David was come to the top of the mount . . . he worshipped" (v. 31 KJV).

And then David saw Hushai, who was the answer to his prayer! Hushai is called "David's friend" (v. 37; 1 Chron. 27:33), which implies he was a friend at court and a special counselor to the king. He was an Arkite, which means he came from a group of people who descended from Canaan and thus were Gentiles (Gen. 10:17; 1 Chron. 1:15). The town of Arka was located in Syria, about two hundred miles north of Damascus and five miles east of the sea. David's conquests had reached that far north, and some of the people had begun to worship the true God of Israel and to serve the king.

As he had done with Zadok and Abiathar and their two sons, so David did with Hushai: he sent him back to Jerusalem to "serve" Absalom. All five men were taking risks for the sake of the Lord and the kingdom, but they considered it an honor to serve their king and help restore him to the throne. All of the people to whom David gave special assignments could say, "We are your servants, ready to do whatever my lord the king commands" (v. 15 NKJV). This would be a fine statement for believers to adopt today as an expression of their devotion to Christ.

Hushai came to Jerusalem just as Absalom arrived, and the people's excitement at greeting the new king probably enabled Hushai to enter the city without being noticed, or perhaps he strengthened his position by joining the crowd. Of course, later Hushai would greet the king and go to work doing all he could to obstruct his plans and keep David informed. If there's one thing better than *getting* an answer to prayer it's *being* an answer to prayer, and Hushai was the answer to David's prayer. Humanly speaking, were it not for Hushai's counsel to Absalom, David might have been slain in the wilderness.

The Lord meets David's needs (16:1-4). When David met Hushai, it was an answer to prayer, but when he met Ziba, the encounter met an immediate need but created a problem that wasn't settled until David returned to the throne. Ziba had been one of Saul's land managers as well as a custodian of Jonathan's crippled son Mephibosheth (chap. 9). Knowing that Ziba was an opportunist with evil motives, David was suspicious about Ziba's presence, his gifts, and the absence of Mephibosheth, who had been cared for by David. Ziba had brought a string of donkeys (NIV) for David and his family to use, as well as generous amounts of bread, wine, and fruit. The gifts were needed and appreciated, but David was concerned about the motive behind them.

Ziba lied to the king and did his best to discredit his young master Mephibosheth. David was weary and deeply wounded within, and it wasn't the best time for him to be making character decisions. He accepted Ziba's story—which was later discredited (19:26-27)—and made a rash judgment that gave Ziba the property that rightfully belonged to Mephibosheth. "He who answers a matter before he hears it, it is folly and shame to him"

(Prov. 18:13). God's leaders must constantly be on guard lest they make unwise decisions on the basis of incomplete information.

God honors David's submission (16:5-14). Through Ziba's lies, Satan attacked David as a serpent who deceives (2 Cor. 11:3; Gen. 3:1-7), and then through Shimei's words and stones, Satan came as a lion who devours (1 Peter 5:8). Ziba told lies and Shimei threw stones, and both were making it hard for David. The king was now near Bahurim[8] in the tribe of Benjamin, where the pro-Saul forces were still strong. Shimei was on the hillside opposite David and above him, and it was easy for him to throw stones and clumps of dirt at David and his people. David was exhausted and discouraged, and yet he never rose to greater heights than when he allowed Shimei to go on attacking him. Abishai was only too willing to cross over and kill the man who was attacking the king, but David wouldn't allow it. Abishai had also wanted to kill Saul in the camp of Israel (1 Sam. 26:6-8), and he assisted his brother Joab in murdering Abner (2 Sam. 3:30), so David knew that his words were not to be treated lightly.

"Get out, get out, you man of blood, you scoundrel!" shouted Shimei, but David didn't retaliate. Shimei was blaming David for the death of Saul and his sons, for after all, David was officially in the Philistine army when they died. The fact that David was miles away from the battlefield when their deaths occurred didn't seem to matter to Shimei. This loyal Benjamite probably blamed David for the death of Saul's son Ish-Bosheth, who inherited Saul's throne, and also Abner, Saul's loyal commander; and, of course, Uriah the Hittite as well. "You have come to ruin because you are a man of blood!" (v. 8). Shimei was breaking the law while giving vent to his hatred of David, for Exodus 22:28 says, "You shall not revile God, nor curse a ruler of your people" (NKJV).

David's attitude was one of submission because he accepted Shimei's abuse as from the hand of God. David had already announced that he would accept anything the Lord sent to him (15:26), and now he proved it. When David considered that he was an adulterer and a murderer who deserved to die, yet God let him live, why should he complain about some stones and dirt?

And if Absalom, David's own son, was out to kill him, why should a total stranger be punished for slandering the king and throwing things at him? David had faith that God would one day balance the books and take care of people like Absalom and Shimei. Perhaps David was thinking of Deuteronomy 32:35: "It is mine to avenge; I will repay" (NIV; see Rom. 14:17-21). When David regained the throne, he pardoned Shimei (19:16-23) and later Solomon restricted him to Jerusalem where he could be watched. When Shimei arrogantly overstepped his bounds, he was arrested and executed (1 Kings 2:36-46).

David and the people went beyond Behurim some twenty miles to the ford of the Jordan River, possibly near Gilgal or Jericho, and there they rested. Very early the next morning they crossed the river and proceeded to Mahanaim (17:22, 24), where Jacob had prepared to meet his brother Esau and had wrestled with God (Gen. 32). Perhaps David remembered that event and gained courage as he thought of the army of angels that God sent to protect Jacob.

What did all this suffering accomplish for David? *It made him more like Jesus Christ!* He was rejected by his own people and betrayed by his own familiar friend. He gave up everything for the sake of the people and would have surrendered his own life to save his rebellious son who deserved to die. Like Jesus, David crossed the Kidron and went up Mount Olivet. He was falsely accused and shamefully treated, and yet he submitted to the sovereign will of God. "[W]ho, when He was reviled, did not revile in return; when He suffered, He did not threaten, but committed Himself to Him who judges righteously" (1 Peter 2:23 NKJV).

David had lost his throne, but Jehovah God was still on the throne and would keep His promises with His servant. Faithful to His covenant, the Lord remembered David and all the hardships that he endured (Ps. 132:1), and He remembers us today.

EIGHT

David's Bittersweet Victory

When General Douglas MacArthur spoke before the United States Congress on April 19, 1951, he made the famous statement, "In war there is no substitute for victory." But more than one military expert has maintained that armed forces can only win battles and that in the long run, nobody really wins a war. Why? Because the price is too high. For every word in Hitler's book *Mein Kampf*, 125 people died in World War II. In view of modern atomic weapons, nobody would "win" World War III.

David's army and Absalom's army were about to engage in battle in a civil war that neither father nor son could "win," but both sides could lose. If David won, it meant death for his son Absalom and his friend Ahithophel; if Absalom won, it could mean death for David and other members of his family. In modern terms, it was a "catch-22" situation; in ancient terms, it would be a "pyrrhic victory."[1]

Absalom was trusting his charm, his popularity, his army, and the wisdom of Ahithophel, but David was trusting the Lord. "Hear my cry, O God; attend to my prayer. From the end of the earth I will cry to You, when my heart is overwhelmed; lead me to the rock that is higher than I" (Ps. 61:1-2 NKJV).

What did David experience during those difficult days?

1. David's throne was usurped (2 Sam. 16:15-23)

This paragraph picks up the narrative that was interrupted at 15:37 so we could learn about David's escape and his encounters with Ziba and Shimei. Thanks to David's speedy departure, Absalom's rebellion was a bloodless coup and he took Jerusalem unopposed, which was just what David wanted (15:14). Unlike Absalom, David was a man with a shepherd's heart who thought first about the welfare of his people (24:17; Ps. 78:70-72).

Hushai won Absalom's confidence (vv. 16-19). As soon as possible, Hushai entered the king's audience chamber and officially presented himself to the new king. He didn't want Absalom to think he was a spy, although that's exactly what he was. He was God's man in Jerusalem to frustrate the counsel of Ahithophel. Absalom was no doubt surprised to see his father's counselor in Jerusalem, but his sarcastic greeting didn't upset Hushai, who spoke respectfully to him. Hushai's words to Absalom must be read very carefully or they will be misunderstood.

Hushai gave the usual respectful greeting "God save the king," *but he didn't say "King Absalom."* In his heart, he was referring to King David, but the new king didn't understand what Hushai was saying. In his pride, Absalom thought Hushai was calling him the king. Again, note that Hushai doesn't mention Absalom's name or say that he will serve the new king. In verse 18, Hushai is speaking about David, for the Lord had never chosen Absalom to be Israel's king; and Hushai didn't promise to serve Absalom but to serve "in the presence" of David's son. In other words, Hushai would be in the presence of Absalom, *but he would be serving the Lord and David.* A proud man, Absalom interpreted Hushai's words to apply to himself, and he accepted Hushai as another counselor. This decision was of the Lord and prepared the way for Absalom's defeat.

Absalom followed Ahithophel's counsel (vv. 20-23). Absalom had two important tasks to perform before he could rule the kingdom of Israel. The first was that he had to seize his father's throne and let it be known that he was officially the king. Unlike his father David, who sought the mind of the Lord through the Urim and Thummim or from a prophet, Absalom looked to human experience and wisdom—and from a human point of view, Ahithophel was among the very best. However, Ahithophel didn't seek the mind of the Lord nor did he want the will of the Lord. His primary goal was to avenge himself against David for the sin he had committed against his granddaughter Bathsheba and her husband Uriah the Hittite.

It was customary for a new king to inherit the previous king's wives and harem, so when Absalom followed Ahithophel's counsel, he was declaring that he was now king of Israel (see 3:7, 12:8 and 1 Kings 2:22). By taking his father's concubines, Absalom was making himself totally abhorrent to his father and breaking down every possible bridge for reconciliation. The new king was telling his followers that there was no turning back and the revolution would continue. But unwittingly, he was doing even more: he was fulfilling Nathan's prophecy that David's wives would be violated in public (12:11-12). David had been on the roof of his house when he lusted after Bathsheba (11:2-4), and that's where David's wives would be violated.

2. David's prayer was answered (2 Sam. 17:1-28)

Having achieved his first purpose and taken over the royal authority, Absalom now had to deal with the second matter and make sure that David and his followers didn't return and take back the kingdom. The solution was simple but drastic: he had to find his father and kill him. For guidance, Absalom turned to his two counselors for help.

Hushai's counsel prevailed (vv. 1-14).[2] Humanly speaking, if Absalom had followed Ahithophel's plan, David would have been slain and Absalom's problems solved. But David had prayed that God would turn Ahithophel's counsel into foolishness (15:31), and God used Hushai to do just that. Note that Ahithophel put himself front and center by using phrases like

"Let me now choose . . . I will arise . . . I will come . . ." and so on. He wanted to be the general of the army because he wanted personally to supervise the murder of his enemy King David. His plan was a good one: use a small army that could move swiftly, attack suddenly at night, and have David's death as the one great goal. Ahithophel would then bring back David's followers and they would swear loyalty to the new king. It would be a quick victory and very little blood would be shed.

Hushai wasn't in the room when Ahithophel outlined his plan, so Absalom called him in and told him what his favorite counselor had said. Directed by the Lord, Hushai took an entirely different approach and focused on the ego of the young king. Hushai's reply isn't a series of "I will" statements about himself but rather a series of statements about the new king that couldn't help but ignite Absalom's imagination and inflate his ego. Hushai laid an effective verbal trap, and Absalom fell into it.

First, Hushai explained why Ahithophel's counsel wasn't wise "at this time," although it had been wise at other times (vv. 7-10). As for focusing only on the murder of David, Absalom knew that his father was a great tactician and a mighty warrior, surrounded by experienced soldiers who feared nothing. All of them were angry because they'd been driven from their homes. They were like a bear robbed of her cubs. (Hushai is a master of metaphor!) Furthermore, David was too smart to stay with the troops; he would hide in a safe place where he couldn't be trapped. His men would be on guard and would set ambushes and kill anybody who came near. David's army was too experienced in war to be unprepared for a sudden attack. A sudden attack by a small army would not work. If the invading army were repulsed, word would spread that Absalom's forces had been defeated, and then all his men would flee. Absalom would then begin and end his reign with a military disaster.

Then Hushai presented a plan that overcame all these difficulties. First, the new king himself must lead the army, and it must be the biggest army he could assemble "from Dan to Beersheba." This suggestion appealed to Absalom's inflated ego, and in his imagination he could see himself leading the army to a great victory. Of course, he wasn't a seasoned military man, but what difference did that make? What a way to begin his reign! Absalom didn't stop to consider that it would take time to gather his forces "from Dan to Beersheba," time that David could use to cross the Jordan River and "get lost." Hushai, of course, was interested in buying time for David so he could "get lost."

With such a large army at his command, Absalom didn't have to depend on a difficult surprise attack but could "fall on" David's men over a wide area, like the morning dew that falls on the ground. Wherever David's men fled, they would see Absalom's forces and there would be no escape. Instead of sparing David's forces, Absalom's army would wipe them out so they couldn't cause trouble in the future. Realizing that Absalom might be worried about the time element, Hushai answered his objections in verse 13. If during the delay in rounding up his troops Absalom heard that David had taken his men into a walled city, the task would be even easier. The whole nation would obey their new king and work together taking the city apart, stone by stone! What a demonstration of power!

Ahithophel's matter-of-fact speech was forgotten as Hushai's grand plan, punctuated with vivid mental pictures, gripped the hearts and minds of Absalom and his leaders. God had answered David's prayer and confused the counsel of Ahithophel. Absalom would ride at the front of his army, intent on victory, but he would meet with humiliating defeat. "The Lord brings the counsel of the nations to nothing; He makes the plans of the peoples of no effect. The counsel of the Lord stands forever, the plans of His heart to all generations" (Ps. 33:10-11 NKJV).

David's spy system worked (vv. 15-22). David and his people were camped at the fords of the Jordan, about twenty miles from Jerusalem, and the two runners were waiting at En Rogel in the Kidron Valley, less than a mile from Jerusalem. Hushai gave the message to the two priests and told them to tell David to cross over the Jordan as quickly as possible. He was not to delay. If Absalom changed his mind and adopted Ahithophel's plan, then all might be lost. Zadok and Abiathar told an anonymous maid-servant; she took the message to Jonathan and Ahimiaaz, who immediately ran a mile south to the house of a collaborator in Bahurim. However, a young man saw them leave and recognized the priests' sons. Wanting to impress the new king, he told Absalom what was happening, and Absalom's guards started out after the two young men.

At this point, the account reads like the story of the two spies recorded in Joshua 2. Rahab hid the two spies under stalks of flax on the roof of her house. The wife in Bahurim hid the two run-ners in a cistern, covered the opening with a cloth, and sprinkled grain on the cloth. The cloth looked like it was there to provide a place to dry grain in the sun. Not obligated to assist Absalom in his evil plans, the woman sent the guards off in the wrong direction, and the young men were saved. They arrived at David's camp, gave the king the facts, and urged him to cross the Jordan immediately, which he did. The guards returned to Jerusalem empty-handed, but Absalom didn't see their failure as a serious problem. How wrong he was!

Ahithophel took his own life (v. 23). Why? Was it because Absalom hurt his feelings by rejecting his counsel? No, it was because he knew that Hushai's counsel would bring about Absalom's defeat, and Ahithophel was serving the wrong king. As a traitor against King David, Ahithophel would either be slain or banished forever from the kingdom. Rather than humil-iate himself and his family in his death, he put his affairs in order and hanged himself. His suicide reminds us of what Judas did (Matt. 27:5) and points to what David had written in two of his wilderness psalms (Pss. 41:9; 55:12-15; see John 13:18). In Acts 1:15-22, Peter referred to two other psalms that concerned Judas (Pss. 69:25 and 109:8).

Ahithophel had been a faithful servant of the king and the kingdom until he determined in his heart to get vengeance on David for what he did to Bathsheba and Uriah. This desire for revenge so obsessed him that he ceased to be a servant of the Lord and began to serve his own sinful desires. He knew of

Absalom's ambitions but kept them hidden from David, and he cooperated with the crown prince in the palace coup. But with all of his wisdom, Ahithophel was supporting the wrong king, and the Lord had to judge him. Both Ahithophel and Absalom ended up hanging from a tree. How tragic it is when a man or woman leads an exemplary and useful life and then fails dishonorably at the end. There are old fools as well as young fools, and Ahithophel was one of them. All of us need to pray that the Lord will help us to end well.

Friends cared for David (vv. 24-29). David and his party forded the river and came to Mahanaim, the former capital of the ten tribes when Saul's son Ish-Bosheth was king (2:8). It was at Mahanaim ("two camps, two hosts") that Jacob saw the army of angels God had sent to protect him (Gen. 32), but David had no such vision. However, God often uses human "angels" to help His servants, and this time it was Shobi, Machir, and Barzillai. They brought provisions for the king and his people and saw to it that were adequately cared for. God prepared a table for David as his enemies were approaching (Ps. 23:5).

Absalom's army was commanded by Amasa, who was David's nephew and Joab's cousin (v. 25). Of course, Absalom was commander in chief (17:11). How sad that son was fighting against father, uncle against nephew, cousin against cousin, and citizen against citizen. War is bad enough, but a civil war makes an even worse war. Absalom and his men crossed the Jordan, intending to meet David's army somewhere near the forest of Ephraim, about three miles northwest of Mahanaim. The forest of Ephraim was probably named by some Ephraimites who crossed the river and settled on the western side in the region of Gilead.

3. David's son was slain (2 Sam. 18:1-18)

Knowing that the enemy was soon to arrive, David numbered his troops, divided them into three companies, and placed Joab, Abishai, and Ittai as their commanders. Whatever approach Absalom and Amasa used, David's men would be able to maneuver and help each other. David offered to accompany the army, but the people told him to stay in a place of safety in the walled city. (See 21:15-17, which occurred long before Absalom's rebellion.) "There are ten thousand of us but only one of you!" they argued. They knew that Absalom's soldiers would go after the king and not worry about the soldiers. If David stayed in the city, he could send our reinforcements if they were needed. David accepted their decisions; he didn't want to fight his son anyway.

But neither did he want the army to fight his son! Absalom had stood at the gate in Jerusalem and attacked his father (15:1-6); now David stood at a city gate and instructed the soldiers to go easy on Absalom. Absalom certainly hadn't been gentle with his father! He had murdered Amnon, driven David out of Jerusalem, seized his throne, violated David's concubines, and now he was out to kill David. That doesn't sound like the kind of man you would want to protect, but if David had one fault, it was pampering his sons (1 Kings 1:5-6; see 1 Sam. 3:13). But before we criticize David, we must remember that he was a man after God's own heart. Let's be thankful that our Father in heaven hasn't dealt with us according to our sins (Ps. 103:1-14). In His grace, He gives us what we don't deserve, and in His mercy He doesn't give us what we do deserve. Jesus didn't deserve to die, for He was sinless; yet He took the punishment that belonged to us. What a Savior!

The battle spread out across the area, and many soldiers died because of the density of the forest. We don't know how many men perished on each side, but it's likely that most of the ten thousand dead belonged Absalom's army. Both the sword and the forest devoured their victims. (This metaphor has been used before in 1:22 and 2:26.) But God didn't need a sword to stop the rebel Absalom; He simply used the branch of a tree! How much his heavy head of hair contributed to this accident isn't recorded, but it's ironic that the thing he was so proud of (14:25-26) turned out to assist in his death. Indeed, pride does lead to judgment. Another example is Samson (Jud. 16). "He catches the wise in their own craftiness, and the counsel of the cunning comes quickly upon them" (Job 5:13 NKJV).

The soldiers who encountered Absalom hanging from the tree didn't dare touch him, but Joab had his own agenda. It was Joab who had orchestrated the reconciliation of David and Absalom, and now Joab ignored David's orders and killed the young man. Absalom rejected Ahithophel's plan to "kill the king only," but Joab accepted it! There's a hint in verse 11 that Joab had quietly spread the word that he would reward any soldier who killed the rebellious son. The soldier who could have won the reward refused to kill Absalom for two reasons: he didn't want to disobey the king, and he wasn't sure Joab would defend him if the king found out about it. After all, David killed the man who said he killed Saul (1:1-16) as well as the two men who killed Saul's son Ish-Bosheth (4:1ff). The soldier knew that Joab didn't want to be caught issuing an order to kill the king's son when the king commanded otherwise. The death of Absalom marked the end of the war and the rebellion, so Joab withdrew his troops.

Both Absalom and Ahithophel died on trees, and to an Israelite, hanging a body on a tree was evidence that the deceased was cursed by God (Deut. 21:22-23; Gal. 3:13). When you consider the crimes these two men committed, is it any wonder they were cursed? Yet God in His grace forgave David of the same crimes and allowed him to live. At one time, Absalom was the most popular man in the kingdom, but he ended up being buried in a pit, his body covered with stones. Apparently his three sons had died (14:27), so there was no one left in his family to perpetuate his name; so he erected a pillar to keep his name alive (v. 18). Even the original pillar is gone, and the so-called Tomb of Absalom seen today in the Kidron Valley is from the days of the Herods. "The memory of the righteous is blessed, but the name of the wicked will rot" (Prov. 10:7 NKJV).

4. David's heart was broken (2 Sam. 18:19-33)

The war was over and the rebellion ended. All that remained was for Joab to notify the king and return him safely to Jerusalem. But it was a bittersweet victory for David. When the enemy is your own son, there can be no triumph and no celebration.

Ahimaaz was a well-known runner (v. 27), and he volunteered to take the news to the king at Mahanaim, some three miles away. As enthusiastic as the young man was, he didn't realize what he was asking; for David was known to take out his anger and sorrow on the messengers (1:4-16; 4:8-12)! Although the word "tidings" that Ahimaaz used could apply to any kind of news, it usually referred to "good news," and there was no good news that day. Joab knew his king very well and knew that the report of Absalom's death must be conveyed with compassion and skill. To keep Ahimaaz safe, Joab selected a person known only as "the Cushite," who was possibly one of his own servants. Better that a foreign servant be slain than the son of a Jewish priest. However, after the Cushite left, Ahimaaz continued to annoy Joab and ask for permission to run. There was nothing good or bad to add to the news, so why run? Weary of hearing the young man's pleas, Joab gave him permission to go.

Ahimaaz reminds us of those bothersome people who want to be important but have nothing much to say. He took the long, easy route to Mahanaim through the valley, while the Cushite took the short, direct route over difficult terrain. Ahimaaz was a young man without a real message or the ability to convey that message in the right way. As the Cushite ran, he meditated on how to tell King David that his son was dead. What's the sense in running if you don't know how to share the news?

The scene shifts to Mahanaim where David is seated between the outer and inner gates of the city, waiting for the watchman in the tower to give him word that a messenger is on his way from the battlefield.[4] Even though he was unprepared to speak to the king, Ahimaaz put forth every effort and passed the Cushite on the road. David said, "He is a good man. He comes with good news" (v. 27 NIV). It's obvious that the character of the messenger has nothing to do with the contents of the message, but David was grasping for any straw of hope available.

Before he arrived at the gate, Ahimaaz was so anxious to give the news that he called out, "All is well."[5] Then he came to the king, bowed before him and told him that Joab had won the battle. When David asked about Absalom, the young messenger was not prepared or equipped to share the bad news, so he made an excuse that was undoubtedly a lie. In his feeble attempt to go down in history as the man who brought the news from the forest of Ephraim to Mahanaim, Ahimaaz ended up having nothing to say that David wanted to hear. What he said was correct, but he didn't say enough. He ended up standing to one side and watching the Cushite deliver the right message in the right way.

During my pastoral ministry, I've occasionally had to be the bearer of bad news. I can recall praying, pondering, and putting myself in the place of the waiting people, all the while trying to assemble words that would bring the least amount of hurt. It wasn't easy. Someone has defined "tact" as "the knack of making a point without making an enemy," and the Cushite had tact.

The text says that David "trembled violently" when he comprehended that Absalom had been slain. No doubt he had prayed that the worst would not happen, but it happened just the same. In one sense, David pronounced his own sentence when he said to Nathan, "And he shall restore the lamb fourfold" (12:5), for this was the final payment of David's great debt. The baby had died, Tamar was raped, Amnon was slain and now Absalom was dead. David tasted once again the pain of forgiven sin.

But David's tears reveal the broken heart of a loving father. Speaking about David's sorrow, Charles Spurgeon said, "[I]t would be wise to sympathize as far as we can, than to sit in judgment upon a case which has never been our own."[6] David wept when he heard about the death of Jonathan and Saul (1:11-12), the murder of Abner (3:32), and the murder of Amnon (13:33-36), so why shouldn't he weep over the death of his beloved son Absalom? Once again, we see the heart of God revealed in the heart of David, for Christ died for us when we were sinners and living as the enemies of God (Rom. 5:7-10). David would have died for Absalom, but Jesus *did die for us!*

David's problem wasn't that he grieved over his son, for grief is a very human response and tears are a part of the healing. His problem was that he grieved excessively and wouldn't permit himself to be comforted. His response was abnormal. He neglected himself and his responsibilities and had to be soundly rebuked by Joab before he would take steps to return to Jerusalem and save the kingdom. His troubles weren't over, but the Lord would empower him to be the ruler He wanted him to be.

The Lord can heal a broken heart, if we give all the pieces to Him and obey Him by faith.

NINE

David's Return and Renewed Problems

The repeated theme in this chapter is "bringing back the king" (vv. 10, 11, 12, 15, 41). David was across the Jordan in Mahanaim, but he belonged in Jerusalem. All the tribes, including David's own tribe of Judah, had participated in Absalom's rebellion to some extent; now it was time for them to bring their king back to Jerusalem. Years of intrigue and intertribal conflict left Israel a deeply divided nation, and there was a desperate need for a strong display of unity and loyalty. This chapter describes five steps David took to bring about the healing of the nation.

1. David focuses his perspective (19:1-8)

The saintly Scottish pastor Andrew Bonar (1810–1892) used to say, "Let us be as watchful after the victory as before the battle." It's possible to win the battle but lose the victory, which is what happened to David after Joab defeated Absalom and his army. What should have been a day of celebration for David's army at Mahanaim became a confused time of embarrassment and shame as the people[1] stole back into the city as if they had been humiliated by defeat. They had risked their lives for king and country, and were now treated like criminals!

It was very unlike David to be insensitive to the sacrifices his men made as they served him (see 23:13-17; 1 Sam. 30:21-30), but that day he was so obsessed with the death of Absalom that he could think of nothing else. By isolating himself from his men, the king turned a military victory into an emotional defeat. David was not only a great warrior but also a deeply emotional poet and musician, a man who could go from the depths of despair into the heights of glory while writing one psalm. David had experienced a difficult time after the death of Amnon (13:37-39), and the death of his favorite son Absalom left him inconsolable. David's attitude puzzled his followers, who saw Absalom as a liar, a murderer, a traitor, and a rebel.

Certainly we expect a father to grieve over the tragic death of a son and overlook the son's mistakes and sins. But leaders must still lead, even if their hearts are broken; that's one of the prices that leaders must pay. On October 10, 1950, Sir Winston Churchill was introduced at the University of Copenhagen as "the architect of victory" in World War II. Churchill replied: "I was only the servant of my country and had I, at any moment, failed to express her unflinching resolve to fight and conquer, I should at once have been rightly cast aside." David the father forgot that he was also David the king and that he still had his crown because his brave soldiers put the good of the nation ahead of their own personal interests.

Joab's short but cutting speech jolted the king back to reality, and David took his place at the gate—where his men came to him and where he acknowledged their brave service. It's likely that David didn't yet know that it was Joab who engineered Absalom's death and burial, otherwise his response might have been different. It didn't take long for David to find out what Joab and his men did and this helped to precipitate David's naming Amasa as general of the army (v. 13; and see 1 Kings 2:5).

The one thing that's missing in the entire Absalom episode is David's seeking the mind of the Lord as he made decisions. The younger David called for the Urim and Thummim or asked for the counsel of a prophet, but apart from his prayer in 15:31, we don't find David requesting guidance. Of course, the wilderness psalms record his concerns and prayers, so we know he wasn't depending on himself and his leaders alone. But we wish David had sought God's direction as he dealt with Absalom and the problems he created. When it came to dealing with his sons, David needed all the help he could get, but perhaps he wouldn't admit it. It's never too late for God to work.

2. David strives for unity (2 Sam. 19:9-15)

When David finally arrived in Jerusalem, it was a signal to the nation that the rebellion was ended and their true king was back on the throne. But en route to Jerusalem, David made some royal decisions that sent out other important messages to the people. His first message was that he wanted his kingdom to be a united people. The old prejudices and animosities must be buried and the nation must be united behind their king. Within the tribes the people were divided between the followers of Absalom and the followers of David (vv. 9-10), and the old division between "the ten tribes (Israel) and Judah" still persisted (vv. 40-43).

David began with Judah (vv. 11-12). The leaders from all twelve tribes should have united in sending a formal invitation to David to return and reign, but party squabbles and tribal friction kept things in ferment. David knew that the trouble would only increase if he waited too long to regain his city and his throne, so he marched right ahead. After all, he was God's anointed king (v. 22) and didn't need to call for a referendum before taking up his fallen scepter.

Judah was the royal tribe (Gen. 49:10), David was from the tribe of Judah, his capital city was in Judah, and it was the elders of Judah who had first made him king (2:1-4), so he logically turned first to the elders of Judah for help. Using his two priests as intermediaries, David told the elders of Judah that the Israelites in the other tribes were talking about returning the king to Jerusalem, but he had heard nothing from his own tribe. Absalom had begun his rebellion in Hebron, which was in Judah, and the leaders of Judah must have cooperated with him, so it was time they displayed their allegiance to David, their rightful king. It's likely that all the tribal leaders who had foolishly followed Absalom were wondering what David would do to them once he regained his throne.

David appointed Amasa to be his general (vv. 13-14). The news of this appointment must have shocked the leaders of the nation and then brought them great relief, for it meant that David was pardoning all the officials who had followed Absalom. Amasa had been Absalom's general whose assignment it was to search for David and destroy him, but now David was making his nephew (and Joab's cousin) the leader of his great army.

But why replace Joab? For one thing, David learned that it was Joab who had slain Absalom in disobedience to the orders the king had given. Even though he deserved death, Absalom could have been taken alive and brought to David to be dealt with later; and Joab didn't have the authority to defy his sovereign and act as judge and executioner. If Joab did this to the king's son, what might he do to the king himself? This brings up a second reason David replaced Joab: Joab had been gradually increasing his authority ever since David had been told to stop waging war personally (21:15-17).

In the ancient East, the king was commander in chief of the army, and whoever took his place, for whatever reason, became a man of high esteem and authority. It was Joab who told David to come to Rabbah for the final conquest; otherwise, Joab would take the city and name it after himself! By the time of the battle of the forest of Ephraim, Joab had at least ten armor-bearers (18:15)! Joab had a record of eliminating anybody who threatened his authority. He and his brother Abishai killed Abner, who had been King Saul's general (3:27ff); and before the story ends, Joab will kill Amasa (20:4-13).

Joab and his brothers, though capable warriors, caused much grief to David from the early in his reign (3:39; 16:10; 19:22). Of course, Joab knew all about the murder of Uriah (11:14ff), and perhaps this piece of information carried more power than his sword. When he killed Absalom, Joab went too far, and David saw this as an opportunity to get rid of his power-hungry general. Amasa had led the rebel army, so by appointing him to Joab's position, David united the army and declared an amnesty to all the rebel soldiers, giving the nation a new beginning.

As the other tribes debated and delayed, the men of Judah united behind David with all their hearts, and they sent him an official invitation to return home. David went down to the Jordan near Gilgal, and the men of Judah met him there. The first place Israel camped after Joshua had led them across the Jordan, Gilgal was less than twenty miles from Jerusalem and a key city in Jewish history. There the males of the new generation entered into covenant with Jehovah and were circumcised (Josh. 3–5), and it was at Gilgal that Samuel renewed the covenant when Saul became king (1 Sam. 11:14-15). The text doesn't state it, but perhaps David also renewed the covenant at Gilgal and assured the people that Jehovah was still on the throne and His Word was still in force. Perhaps it was a time of rededication for the king, for throughout the rest of the book, we see David very much in charge.

3. David declares general amnesty (2 Sam. 19:16-23)

Not only were the men of Judah at the Jordan to welcome David, but his enemy Shimei the Benjamite was there[2] with a thousand men from his tribe (see 16:5-14). Ziba, the land manager for Mephibosheth (9:1-10), was also in the crowd with his fifteen sons and twenty servants, and they crossed the river to meet him on the western shore and help escort him to the other side. Somebody provided a ferryboat that went back and forth across the Jordan to carry the king's household so they wouldn't have to ford the river. When David arrived on the western bank of the river, Shimei prostrated himself and begged for mercy.

There's no doubt that Shimei deserved to be killed for the way he treated David (Ex. 22:28), and Abishai was willing to do the job, but David stopped his nephew just as he had done before (16:9). The first time David stopped Abishai, his reason was that the Lord had told Shimei to curse the king, so David would take his abuse as from the hand of the Lord. But now his reason for sparing Shimei was because it was a day of rejoicing, not a day of revenge. But even more, by pardoning Shimei, King David was offering a general amnesty to all who had supported Absalom during the rebellion.

David kept his word and didn't have Shimei killed for his crime, but when David was about to die, he warned Solomon to keep an eye on Shimei (1 Kings 2:8-9). Solomon put him under house arrest and told him not to leave Jerusalem, but when Shimei disobeyed the king, he was taken and slain (1 Kings 2:36-46). Shimei had a weakness for resisting authority and treating God's appointed ministers with disdain (Jude 8), and that's why David cautioned Solomon. Shimei didn't appreciate David's mercy or Solomon's grace, and his independence and arrogance finally caught up with him.

4. David corrects an error (2 Sam. 19:24-30)

Mephibosheth, the lame prince, had been "adopted" into David's household and permitted to eat at the king's table (9:1ff), a gift from David in honor of Jonathan, Mephibosheth's father and David's beloved friend. When David became king of all Israel, he inherited everything that had belonged to Saul, including his land, and some of the land he turned over to Mephibosheth to help support him and his family. David commanded Saul's servant Ziba to care for both the land and obey Mephibosheth, which he promised to do. But when David was escaping from Jerusalem, Ziba showed up without his master and brought help to David and his people. At that time, David made an impulsive decision and gave all the land to Ziba (16:1-4). Ziba also showed up to help David cross the river and return home (19:17).

Ziba wasn't on hand to help him, so it would have been difficult for the crippled prince to travel the twenty miles or so from Jerusalem to the Jordan, but he did it.[3] He knew that Ziba had slandered him by telling David that he hoped the rebellion would succeed and the crown be returned to the house of Saul. Mephibosheth wanted an opportunity to speak to David personally, deny Ziba's lies, and affirm his own allegiance to the king, all of which he did. The repeated address "my lord the king" came from his heart. He was loyal to the king.

As David listened to Mephibosheth's explanation, he realize that he had jumped to conclusions when he gave all the land to Ziba, but David didn't have time to conduct a hearing to settle the matter. Mephibosheth made it clear that he wasn't asking his king for anything. The king had given him life, so what more was there to desire? To paraphrase his speech, "I have more than I deserve, so why should I seek the throne? I was destined to die and you not only saved me but took me into your own family circle."

David's response isn't easy to understand. On the surface, he seemed to be saying, "There's no need to go into the matter again. You and Ziba divide the land." But was David the kind of man who went back on his word? How would that kind of decision be received by the thousand Benjamites who came to the Jordan to welcome David? After all, doing something kind to Mephibosheth would have strengthened David's ties with both the tribe of Benjamin (Saul's tribe) and also the ten tribes that had originally followed the house of Saul. Taking away half of Mephibosheth's inheritance hardly fit into the joyful and forgiving atmosphere of the day, and yet by dividing the estate, David was also forgiving Ziba of his lies and treachery to his master. By dividing the land between Ziba and Mephibosheth, David was taking the easy way out.

But Mephibosheth's reply must have stunned David: "Rather, let him take it all, inasmuch as my lord the king has come back in peace to his own house" (v. 30 NKJV). But thanks to David's impetuous judgment, Ziba already had it all! This situation reminds us of the "case of the dead baby" that Solomon had to solve (1 Kings 3:16-28). When he offered to divide the living baby, the child's true mother protested, and that's how Solomon discovered her identity. Unlike a living baby, land isn't harmed when it's divided; but perhaps David was testing Mephibosheth to see where his heart was. The text doesn't tell us, but perhaps Mephibosheth did receive all the land as in the original contract.

Either way, the lame prince was cared for as Ziba worked the land.

5. David rewards the faithful (2 Sam. 19:31-40)

Barzillai was one of three wealthy landowners who met David when he arrived at Mahanaim and together supplied his needs and the needs of his people (17:27-29). He returned to his home in Rogelim, twenty to twenty-fives miles north. When he heard that David was returning to Jerusalem, he came down to see him off. Unlike Shimei, he had no sins to confess, nor was there a misunderstanding to straighten out as with Mephibosheth. Barzillai wanted no favor from the king. All he wanted was to have the joy of sending him off safely, knowing that the war was over. These two trips must have been difficult for an eighty-year-old man, but he wanted to give his best to his king.

David wanted to reward Barzillai by caring for him at his palace in Jerusalem. Not only did David want to express his thanks, but by having so important a man in Jerusalem, it would strengthen ties with the trans-Jordanic citizens at a time when unity was an important commodity. But Barzillai graciously refused David's offer on the grounds that he was too old. Older people don't like to pull up their roots and relocate, and they want to die at home and be buried with their loved ones. At his age, Barzillai couldn't enjoy the special pleasures of life at court, and he would only be a burden to the king, who had enough to think about.

However, Barzillai was willing to let his son Chimham take his place (1 Kings 2:7) and go to Jerusalem to live. What Barzillai didn't need for himself he was willing for others to enjoy. Said Matthew Henry, "They that are old must not begrudge young people those delights which they themselves are past the enjoyment of, nor oblige them to retire as they do." Barzillai crossed the river with David and Chimham and went a short distance with them, and then they said good-bye, David affectionately kissing his friend and benefactor.[4] In Jeremiah's time, there was a site known as Geruth Kimham ("habitation of Chimham") near

Bethlehem (Jer. 41:17), which may have been where Barzillai's son settled down with his family.

But David's troubles weren't over yet, for the long-running feud between the ten tribes and Judah would surface again and almost cause another civil war. Shakespeare was right: "Uneasy lies the head that wears a crown."[5]

TEN

David's New Struggles

The humorous poet Ogden Nash was sounding a serious note when he wrote, "People could survive their natural troubles all right if it weren't for the trouble they make for themselves." Ouch!

As we read the account of David's later life, we can see the truth of that statement. All parents have predictable problems with their children, but the sins of David's children seemed to set new records, especially those of Absalom. All leaders have problems with their followers, but in David's case, the sword flashed repeatedly in Israel with brother fighting against brother. How painful are the consequences of forgiven sin! These chapters describe four different conflicts that David had to deal with after Absalom's rebellion had been crushed.

1. Tribal conflict (19:41–20:4, 14-26)

A crisis will bring out the best in some people and the worst in others. The representatives of the tribes were gathered at Gilgal to escort their king back to Jerusalem, and instead of rejoicing at the victory God had given His people, the tribes were fighting among themselves. The "men of Israel" were the ten northern tribes, and they were angry at the southern tribe of Judah, which had also absorbed the tribe of Simeon. Israel was angry because Judah had not waited for them to arrive on the scene to help take David home. Judah had "kidnapped" the king and had ignored and insulted the other ten tribes. Judah replied that David was from their tribe, so they had the greater responsibility to care for him. Israel argued that they had ten shares in David but Judah had only two, as though the king were some kind of security on the stock market. Apparently nobody urged the tribes to call on Jehovah for His help and to remember that Gilgal was the place where Israel had made a new beginning in Joshua's day (Josh. 3–5).

The conflict between Judah and Israel had deep roots, just like the political conflicts that divide many nations today. When King Saul assembled his first army, it was divided between Israel and Judah (1 Sam. 11:8), and this division continued throughout his reign (15:4; 17:52; 18:16). After the death of Saul, the ten tribes of Israel followed Saul's son Ish-Bosheth, while Judah followed David (2 Sam. 2:10-11). Judah, of course, was obeying the will of God, for the Lord had named David as the nation's next king. This tribal rivalry existed even in David's day (11:11; 12:8). "Every kingdom divided against itself is brought to desolation," said Jesus, "and every city or house divided against itself shall not stand" (Matt. 12:25 KJV). When Rehoboam became king after the death of Solomon his father, the rift widened and the kingdom divided into Judah and Israel.

All it takes to light the fires of conflict is a speech from a would-be leader, and Sheba was that leader. Being a Benjamite, he favored the house of Saul, and he was probably an officer in the northern army. If the ten tribes seceded from the kingdom, perhaps he could become commander of their army. Sheba didn't declare war; all he did was dismiss the army and the citizens who came from the northern tribes and tell them not to follow David any longer. But in essence it was a declaration of war, for Sheba marched through the northern tribes trying to gather a following (v. 14). It appears that not many people responded, and Sheba and his followers ended up in the walled city of Abel.

Joab again took command of David's troops and followed Sheba to Abel, surrounded the city, and began to lay siege to it. For the third time in the "David story," a woman changes the course of events. Abigail was the first (1 Sam. 25), and the woman of Tekoa was the second (2 Sam. 14). The wise woman called to Joab from the wall and assured him that her city was not in league with any rebels and therefore didn't deserve to be attacked. Perhaps she was thinking about the law in Deut. 20:10-16 requiring that a city first be given an offer of peace before it was attacked. When Joab explained that it was only Sheba he was after, she persuaded the citizens to kill the rebel leader and save the city. However, Sheba wasn't a scapegoat; as a rebel against the king, he deserved to be slain. Sheba wanted to be head of the army, but instead, his head was thrown over the wall to the army.

The chapter closes with a second listing of David's officers (8:15-18), and two new officers are added: Adoram (or Adoniram) was in charge of the forced labor, and Ira the Jairite served as David's chaplain. The "forced labor" was done by prisoners of war, but Israelites were occasionally conscripted to assist with government building projects. During Solomon's reign and after, the officer in charge of these labor projects didn't have an easy time of it (1 Kings 4:6; 5:14; 12:18ff; 2 Chron. 10:18-19).

Now we must back up a bit to discover how Joab regained the command of David's army.

2. Personal conflict (20:4-13)

When David heard about Sheba's call to rebellion, he immediately sent word to Amasa, his new commander (19:13), to gather the troops within three days and come to Jerusalem. An experienced strategist, David knew that insurrection had to be nipped in the bud or it would gain momentum among the dissatisfied people in the land, and this could lead to another war. Thousands of David's subjects had been willing to follow Absalom, and it seemed that the ten northern tribes were ready to follow anybody.

But Amasa didn't show up with the army within the three allotted days, and David gave the command of the army to Abishai. Amasa had been commander of Absalom's army, so perhaps David was afraid he had turned traitor and joined up with Sheba. The most logical explanation for Amasa's delay was that the men didn't trust him and were unwilling to follow him and risk their lives. Taking Joab's officers and David's "mighty men" with him, Abishai quickly assembled the army of Judah and headed north to stop Sheba. Imagine their surprise when they met Amasa and his army at the great rock in Gibeon, about six miles northwest of Jerusalem. Amasa was on his way to report to David and get his orders.

Though he had no official position, Joab went along with his brother Abishai to help in any way that he could. The two men had fought together in the battle of the forest of Ephraim and defeated Absalom. Joab had no love for Amasa, who had betrayed David and led Absalom's army (17:25). Furthermore, it was Amasa who took Joab's place as commander of the troops, an appointment that must have humiliated Joab. (David made that change because it was Joab who killed Absalom.) Joab knew that he and his brother Abishai could deal successfully with Sheba's revolt but that Amasa was too weak and inexperienced to lead a victorious army.

As when they murdered Abner (3:27-39), Joab and Abishai must have quickly plotted together when they saw Amasa approaching. Joab had killed Abner[1] and Absalom, so his hands were already stained with blood. The trick with the sword gave Amasa the idea that this was just a casual meeting, but it was Joab's crafty way of catching Amasa off-guard. (See Jud. 3:20-23.) Once more, the sword was at work in David's household, for Amasa was his cousin. There was no reason why Amasa should be killed. True, he had joined forces with Absalom, but David had declared a general amnesty that included Joab, who had killed Absalom. Joab could have easily taken the command away from Amasa, but the old campaigner was of such a disposition that he preferred to destroy those who stood in his way. He wanted none of Absalom's leaders to live and create more problems for David.

Joab left Amasa lying in a pool of blood on the highway, a sight that brought the marching army to a halt. Here was their commander dead before the battle had even begun! Joab and Abishai took off after Sheba, but the army wasn't following. It was what we call today "a gaper's block." One of Joab's men was wise enough to move the corpse to the side of the highway and cover it up. Then he rallied Amasa's troops to support Joab and David, and the soldiers responded. The politically correct thing to say would have been "David and Abishai," because David had given the command to Abishai; but Joab had taken back his old position and wouldn't let it go (v. 23). Once again, David had to give in to Joab's power tactics.

We trust that somebody buried the body, for it was considered a serious thing in Israel for a body not to have proper burial.

3. Ethnic conflict (2 Sam. 21:1-14)

The book closes with a record of two national calamities—a drought caused by King Saul's sin (21:1-14) and a plague caused by King David's sin (24:1-25). Between these two tragic events, the writer gives us a summary of four victories (21:15-22) and a list of David's mighty men (23:8-39), as well as two psalms written by David (22:1–23:7). Once again we see David the soldier, the singer, and the sinner.

Sin (vv. 1-4). Nowhere in Scripture are we told when or why Saul slaughtered the Gibeonites and thus broke the vow that Israel had made with them in Joshua's day (Josh. 9). Joshua tried to make the best of his mistake, because he put the Gibeonites to work as woodcutters and water carriers; but Israel's vow obligated them before God to protect the Gibeonites (Josh. 10). Saul killed several Gibeonites but intended to wipe them all out, so it was a case of "ethnic cleansing" and genocide.

Saul's religious life is a puzzle. Attempting to appear very godly, he would make foolish vows that nobody should keep (1 Sam. 14:24-35), while at the same time he didn't obey the clear commands of the Lord (1 Sam. 13, 15). He was commanded to slay the Amalekites and didn't, yet he tried to exterminate the Gibeonites! Another piece of the puzzle is that Jeiel, Saul's great-grandfather, was the progenitor of the Gibeonites (1 Chron. 8:29-33; 9:35-39), so Saul slaughtered his own relatives.

Gibeon became a Levitical city (Josh. 21:17), and the tabernacle was there at one time (1 Kings 3:4-5). The city was located in the tribe of Benjamin—Saul's tribe—and perhaps that is a clue to Saul's behavior. It was bad enough to have the pagan Gibeonites alive and well in the land of Israel, but did they have to reside in Benjamin? One of Saul's "leadership" tactics was to reward his men with houses and lands (1 Sam. 22:7), and perhaps to do this he confiscated property from the Gibeonites. Whatever his motive and method, Saul in his grave brought judgment on the people of Israel as the drought and famine continued for three years (21:1, 10).

The first year of drought might have been caused by some unexpected change in the weather, and during the second year people would say, "It's bound to improve." But when for the third year the land suffered drought and famine, David sought the face of the Lord. It was written in the Lord's covenant with Israel that He would send the rain to the land if His people would honor and obey Him (Deut. 28:1-14). David knew that the sin of murder would pollute the land (Num. 35:30-34), and that's exactly what was causing all the trouble. Perhaps through his prophet Nathan or his chaplain Ira, the Lord said to David, "It is because of Saul and his bloodthirsty house, because He killed the Gibeonites" (v. 1 NKJV). Saul had been dead for over thirty years, and the Lord had patiently waited for this sin to be dealt with.[2]

Retribution (vv. 5-9). When he learned the facts, David immediately offered to make restitution for the terrible sins of his predecessor, because he wanted the Gibeonites to be able to bless the people of Israel and thereby enjoy God's blessing (Gen. 12:1-3). But the Gibeonites didn't want money; they knew that no amount of money could ransom a murderer or recompense the survivors (Num. 35:31-33). The Gibeonites made it clear that they knew their place in Israel as servants and resident aliens, and they had no right to press their case.[3] But it would take the shedding of blood to atone for the Gibeonite blood that had been shed (Ex. 21:24; Lev. 24:19-21; Deut. 19:21). The nation was suffering because of Saul's sins, and if David killed just any man, that wouldn't solve the problem. The Gibeonites asked that seven of Saul's male descendants be sacrificed before the Lord and this would end the drought and famine.

David knew that the Jews were forbidden to offer human sacrifices (Lev. 18:21; 20:1-5; Deut. 12:29-32; 18:10), nor did he see the deaths of the seven men as sacrifices with atoning value. We today who have the New Testament and understand the Gospel of Jesus Christ view this entire episode with mingled disgust and dismay, but we must keep in mind that we're dealing with law, not grace, and Israel, not the church. The Law of Moses required that an unsolved murder be atoned for by sacrifice (Deut. 21:1-9), so how much more a known slaughter perpetrated by a king! However, we must keep in mind that the death of the seven men was not atonement but legal retribution.

Though David didn't commit the crime, he had to choose the seven men who would die, and that wasn't an easy thing to do. (Perhaps David thought about those who had died because of his sin—Bathsheba's baby, Uriah the Hittite, Amnon, Absalom and Amasa.) Because of his vow to Jonathan to protect his descendants (1 Sam. 20:12-17)[4], the king avoided naming Mephibosheth and chose two sons of Saul's concubine Rizpah as well as five sons of Saul's daughter Merab, who was married to Adriel (v. 8 NIV).[5] We aren't told how the seven men were executed, although "fell together" (v. 9) suggests they were pushed off a cliff. This happened during barley harvest in the middle of April, and the seven corpses were exposed for about six months, until the rains arrived and the drought ended in October. To hang up a corpse was to disgrace the person and put him under a curse (Deut. 21:22-23).

Compassion (vv. 10-14). The law required exposed bodies to be taken down by sundown and buried. To be sure that Saul's crime was sufficiently dealt with, David allowed the bodies to remain exposed until the rains came, signifying that the Lord was blessing His people again. During that time Rizpah protected the bodies of her sons and nephews, an act of love and courage. It was Rizpah who was involved when Abner abandoned the house of Saul and joined with David (3:6-12).

But David went a step further. He had the bones gathered up, along with the bones of Saul and his sons that the men of Jabesh-Gilead had interred (1 Sam. 31), and brought the whole family together in their family tomb (vv. 12-14). To have proper burial with one's ancestors was the desire of every Israelite, and David granted this blessing to Saul and his family. Whatever questions remain concerning this unusual event, this much is true: one man's sins can bring sorrow and death to his family, even after he is dead and buried. We must also give credit to David for dealing drastically with sin for the sake of the nation, and yet for showing kindness to the house of Saul.

4. National conflict (21:15-22; 1 Chron. 20:4-8)

These four conflicts took place much earlier in David's reign, probably after he made Jerusalem his capital and the Philistines opposed his rise to power. All four involve "descendants of the giants"[6] from Philistia, one of whom was a brother of Goliath (v. 19).

In the first conflict (vv. 15-17), David fought so much that he grew faint, because the Philistines would focus on him rather than the other soldiers. Ishbi-benob wanted to slay David and had a bronze spear that weighed seven and a half pounds. However David's nephew Abishai, who more than once irritated David, came to the king's rescue and killed the giant. It was then that the military leaders decided the king was too vulnerable and valuable to be sacrificed on the battlefield. The king was the "lamp of Israel" and had to be protected. (See 1 Kings 11:36; 15:4; 2 Kings 8:19; 2 Chron. 21:7.)

The second contest with the Philistines (v. 18; 1 Chron. 20:4) took place at Gob, a site we can't locate with any accuracy, where Israel won the battle because one of David's mighty men killed the giant. (See 1 Chron. 11:29.) The fact that the names of these giants were preserved shows that they were well-known warriors.

The third conflict with the Philistines (v. 19) was again at Gob, and this time the brother of Goliath (1 Chron. 20:5) is the giant that was slain. We know little about Elhanan except that he came from Bethlehem and was one of David's mighty men (23:24).

The fourth battle took place in Gath in enemy territory (vv. 20-22; 1 Chron. 20:6-8), and David's nephew Jonathan killed the giant who had, like Goliath, defied Israel and Israel's God. (See 1 Sam. 17:10.)

When as a youth David killed Goliath, he certainly gave the men of Israel a good example of what it means to trust God for victory. It's good to know how to kill giants yourself, but be sure to help others kill the giants in their lives.

ELEVEN

2 SAMUEL 22
(SEE ALSO PSALM 18)

David's Song of Victory

First Samuel 2 records the song Hannah sang when she brought her son Samuel to serve the Lord at the tabernacle, and 2 Samuel 22 records the song of David after the Lord helped him defeat his enemies (v. 1; Ps.18, title). How significant that two books full of burdens and bloodshed are bracketed by praise! No matter how dark the days or how painful the memories, we can always praise the Lord.

In this song, David offered thanks to the Lord for the many victories He had given him and for the gracious way He had worked to bring him to the throne of Israel. Note that Saul is not included among David's enemies, for no matter what Saul did to him, David never treated Saul like an enemy. It's likely that 2 Samuel 22 is the original version, but when the song was adapted for corporate worship David wrote a new opening: "I will love thee, O Lord, my strength" (Ps. 18:1 KJV). The Hebrew word used here for "love" means "a deep and fervent love," not just a passing emotion. He also deleted from verse 3 "my savior; thou savest me from violence." There are other differences, but they do not deter us from grasping the glorious message of this song of praise.

It's unlikely that this song was written just after the defeat of Saul and the beginning of David's reign in Hebron. From verse

51 we infer that David wrote this psalm after God made His dynastic covenant with him (2 Sam. 7) and gave him the victories recorded in 2 Samuel 8 and 10. We further infer from verses 20-27 that he wrote the psalm before his terrible sins in connection with Bathsheba and Uriah (2 Sam. 11-12), for he could never have written verses 20-27 after that sad episode.

The emphasis in this psalm is on what the Lord in His grace and mercy did for David.

1. The Lord delivered David (2 Sam. 22:1-19)

"Deliver" is a key word in this song (vv. 1, 2, 18, 20, 44, 49), and it carries with it the meanings of "drawing out of danger, snatching, taking away, allowing to escape." For at least ten years before he became king, David was pursued by Saul and his army, and the record shows that Saul tried to kill David at least five times. (See 1 Sam. 18:10-11; 19:8-10, 18-24.) After he became king, David had to wage war against the Philistines, the Ammonites, the Syrians, the Moabites, and the Edomites, and God enabled him to triumph over all his enemies.

David began by praising the Lord for who He is—a rock, a fortress, and a deliverer (v. 20)—images that certainly came out of David's years in the wilderness when he and his men hid in caves and natural fortresses. "God is my rock" (v. 3) can be translated, "My rock-like God." The image of the Lord "the rock" goes back to Genesis 49:24 and is used often in "The Song of Moses" in Deuteronomy 32 (vv. 4, 15, 18, 30-31). Hannah used it in her song (1 Sam. 2:2), and it's found frequently in the psalms. A rock reminds us of strength and stability, that which is dependable and unchanging. No matter how David's enemies tried to destroy him, he was always guided and protected by the Lord. God was a shield around him and a deliverer in every time of danger.

The image of the rock gives way to the image of the flood (vv. 4-7, and this leads to the vivid picture of the storm (vv. 8-20. While he was exiled in the wilderness, David certainly saw many rainstorms (see Ps. 29) that transformed the dry riverbeds into raging torrents (Ps. 126:4). No matter what the season, David was constantly fighting the strong currents of Saul's opposition. Waves of death, floods of ungodly men, the cords of sheol (the land of the dead), and the hidden traps of death all made David's life difficult and dangerous. No wonder he told Jonathan, "There is but a step between me and death" (1 Sam. 20:3 NKJV).

What do you do when you're drowning in a flood of opposition? *You call on the Lord and trust Him for the help you need (v. 7).* David was a man of prayer who depended on the Lord for wisdom, strength, and deliverance, and the Lord never failed him. Why did God wait all those years before delivering David and putting him on the throne? For one thing, the Lord was building himself a leader, and this could be done only by means of trial, suffering, and battle. But the Lord also had his own timetable, for "when the fullness of the time had come" (Gal. 4:4 NKJV), out of David's family the Messiah would come to the world.

When the Lord answered David's cries and delivered him from Saul and the enemies of the people of God, it was like a great thunderstorm being released over the land (vv. 8-20). David describes God's intervention as an earthquake (v. 8) followed by lightning, fire, and smoke (v. 9). The Lord was angry! (See Pss. 74:1 and 140:10.) Against the background of the black sky, the Lord swooped down on a cloud propelled by the cherubim. The storm raged! In Scripture, a storm can picture an advancing army (Ezek. 38:9; Dan. 11:40; Hab. 3:14) or the judgment of God (Jer. 11:6; 23:19; 25:32). God's arrows were like the lightning, His voice like the thunder, and the winds like the angry breath of His nostrils. No wonder His enemies fled in terror! David didn't see himself as a great commander who led a victorious army, but as God's servant who trusted Jehovah to win the victory. He gave all the glory to the Lord. God not only "came down" (v. 10), but He "reached down" and plucked David out of the dangerous waters.

2. The Lord rewarded David (2 Sam. 22:20-28)

For at least ten years, David had been in "tight" places, but now the Lord had brought him out "into a spacious place" (v. 20 NIV). God could give him a larger place because David had been enlarged in his own life through his experiences of trial and testing. "Thou hast enlarged me when I was in distress" (Ps. 4:1 KJV). David had often cried out, "The troubles of my heart are enlarged," but at the same time, God was enlarging His servant and preparing him for a bigger place (18:19, 36). "I called on the Lord in distress; the Lord answered me and set me in a broad place" (Ps. 118:5 NKJV). In the school of life, God promotes those who, in times of difficulty, learn the lessons of faith and patience (Heb. 6:12), and David had learned his lessons well.

David's righteousness (vv. 21-25). A superficial reading of these verses might lead us to believe that David was bragging about himself, but this isn't the case at all. David was praising the Lord for enabling him to live a blameless life in dangerous and uncomfortable situations. Just think of how difficult it would be to keep the law of the Lord in the Judean wilderness while fleeing for your life! In all that he did, David sought to please the Lord, obey His law, and trust His promises. These verses describe David as a man of integrity (see Ps. 78:72), a "man after God's own heart" (1 Sam. 13:14). David knew and claimed God's covenant promises and the Lord honored him. King Saul violated the terms of the covenant, and the Lord judged him.

This doesn't mean that David was spotless and always did the right thing. He had his days of despair when he fled to the enemy for help, but these were incidents in a life that was otherwise wholly devoted to the Lord. David honored only the Lord and never turned to idols. He did not dishonor the name of the Lord; he was careful to love and protect his parents (1 Sam. 22:1-4); and when he had opportunities to slay Saul, David refused to touch the Lord's anointed and commit murder. There is no evidence that during his "battle years" David was a thief, an adulterer, or a false witness against others. (Actually, it was Saul and his men who lied about David.) David was a generous man who didn't cultivate a covetous heart. We don't know how David honored the Sabbath when he was away from the covenant community, but there's no reason to believe that he broke the fourth commandment. Measured by the righteousness of the law, David was a man with clean hands and a pure heart (Ps. 24:3-6), and he received his reward from the Lord.

The Lord's faithfulness (vv. 26-28). The Lord never violates His own attributes. God deals with people according to their attitudes and their actions. David was merciful to Saul and spared his life on at least two occasions, and the Lord was merciful to David. "Blessed are the merciful: for they shall obtain mercy" (Matt. 5:7 KJV). David was faithful to the Lord, and the Lord was faithful to Him. David was upright; he was single-hearted when it came to serving God. He was not sinless—no man or woman on earth is—but he was blameless in his motives and loyal to the Lord. In that sense, his heart was pure: "Blessed are the pure in heart: for they shall see God" (Matt. 5:8 KJV).

Unlike Saul, David was not perverse in heart but submitted to the will of God (v. 27). The NIV reads, "to the crooked you show yourself shrewd," reminding us that faith is living without scheming or making excuses, two practices at which Saul excelled. The Hebrew word translated "froward" (KJV) or "crooked" (NIV) comes from a root that means "to wrestle." David didn't fight God or God's will, but Saul did; and that's why David was exalted but Saul was abased (1 Peter 5:5-6; James 4:10).

Finally, David was humble and broken before the Lord, while Saul promoted himself and put himself first. "You rescue those who are humble, but your eyes are on the proud to humiliate them" (v. 28 NLT). Hannah touched on this important theme in her song to the Lord (1 Sam. 2:3, 7-8). When Saul began his reign, he stood head and shoulders above everybody else (1 Sam. 10:23-24), but at the end of his life, he fell on his face in a witch's house (28:20) and fell as a suicide on the battlefield (31:1-6). "Therefore let him who thinks he stands take heed lest he fall" (1 Cor. 10:12 NKJV). David fell on his face in submission, and the Lord lifted him up in honor. Saul lifted himself up and eventually fell on his face in humiliation.

God is always faithful to His character and His covenant. Knowing the character of God is essential to knowing and doing the will of God and pleasing His heart. David knew God's covenant so he understood what God expected of him. The character of God and the covenant of God are the foundations for the promises of God. If we ignore His character and covenant, we will never be successful in claiming His promises.

3. The Lord enabled David (2 Sam. 22:29-43)

In this stanza of his song, David looked back and recalled how the Lord helped him during those difficult years of exile.

The Lord enlightened David (v. 29). The image of the burning lamp can refer to God's goodness in keeping people alive (Job 18:5-6; 21:17). David's life was constantly in danger, but the Lord kept him alive and provided all he needed. But a burning lamp also speaks of the reign of a king. David's men were afraid that one day he would be slain in battle and the "light of Israel" be put out (2 Sam. 21:17). Even after David died, the Lord was true to His covenant promise and kept David's lamp burning by maintaining David's dynasty (1 Kings 11:36; 15:4; 2 Kings 8:19; 2 Chron. 21:7; Ps. 132:17).

But God enlightened David in another way, for He revealed His will to him through the words of the prophets and the use of the Urim and Thummim. Saul made his own decisions, but David sought the mind of the Lord. During the dark days of his exile, David could say, "The Lord is my light and my salvation; whom shall I fear? The Lord is the strength of my life; of whom shall I be afraid?"[2] (Ps. 27:1 NKJV).

The Lord empowered David (vv. 30-35). The picture here is that of a courageous warrior letting nothing stand in the way of victory. God empowered David to face the enemy without fear, running through a troop and the barricades they put up, and even scaling a wall to take a city. God's way is perfect (v. 31) and He made David's way perfect (v. 33), because David trusted in Him. God shielded David in the battle because David relied wholly on the flawless Word of God.

David's body belonged to the Lord (see Rom. 12:1), and God used his arms, feet and hands (vv. 33-35) to overcome the enemy. David was a gifted warrior, but it was the anointing power of the

Lord that enabled him to succeed on the battlefield. Like a fleet-footed deer, he could reach the heights; even his ankles didn't turn (v. 37 NIV). God made David's arms strong enough to bend a bow of bronze and shoot arrows with great power. In the strength of the Lord, David was invincible.

The Lord enlarged David (vv. 36-43). God enlarged David's path (v. 37) and put him into a larger place (v. 20), a wonderful truth we have already considered. The remarkable statement "thy gentleness hath made me great" (v. 36 KJV) reveals David's utter amazement that Almighty God would condescend to pay any attention to him. David always saw himself as an ordinary Jewish shepherd with no special position in Israel (1 Sam. 18:18, 23), but the Lord "stooped down" to make him great. He made David a great warrior and gave him a great name (2 Sam. 7:23), and David acknowledged this incredible mercy from God, but David's greatest desire was to make Jehovah's name great before the nations (7:18-29).

The gracious condescension of the Lord is a theme that is too often neglected by God's people. As with David, God the Father condescends to work in our lives to fit us for the work of His choosing (and see Isa. 57:15), and God the Son certainly humbled Himself for us when He came to earth as a servant and a sacrifice for sin (Phil. 2:5-11). The Holy Spirit condescended to come to earth and live in the people of God! David didn't look back on those difficult exile years and see the "hardness" of God but the gentleness of God. He saw only goodness and mercy following him (Ps. 23:6). The servant in the parable who called the master "a hard man" (Matt. 25:24) certainly didn't have the same outlook as King David!

We might cringe as we read David's description of his victories, but we must remember that he was fighting the battles of the Lord. If these nations had defeated and destroyed Israel, what would happen to God's great plan of salvation? We wouldn't have a Bible, and we wouldn't have a Savior! In rebelling against the Lord and worshiping idols, these pagan nations had sinned against a flood of light, so they were without excuse (Rom. 1:18ff;

Josh. 2). The Lord had been patient with them for many years (Gen. 15:16), but they had spurned His grace. David pursued his enemies when they tried to get away (vv. 38, 41); he defeated them, crushed them, and ground them into the dirt! They became like mire in the streets.

4. The Lord established David (2 Sam. 22:44-51)

It is one thing to fight wars and defeat the enemy, but it is quite something else to keep these nations under control. David not only had to unify and lead the twelve tribes of Israel, but he also had to deal with the nations that were subjected to Israel.

The Lord enthroned David (44-46). The Gentile nations didn't want a king on the throne of Israel, especially a brilliant strategist, brave warrior, and beloved leader like David. However, God not only established him on the throne, but also promised him a dynasty that would never end. The Lord promised David a throne, and He kept His promise. He also helped David to unite his own people and deal with those who were still loyal to Saul. The word "strangers" in verses 45-46 (KJV) means "foreigners" and refers to Gentile nations. The Lord's victories frightened these peoples and drove them into hiding places. Eventually they would come out of their feeble fortresses and submit to David.

The Lord exalted David (vv. 47-49). David's shout of praise, "The Lord lives" (v. 47), was his bold witness to these subjected peoples that their dead idols could not save them or protect them (see Ps. 115). Only Jehovah, the God of Israel, is the true and living God, and David's victories and enthronement proved that God was with him. David was always careful not to exalt himself, but to exalt the Lord. David closes his song with high and holy praise for the Lord God of Israel. He exalted the Lord, and the Lord exalted him (Matt. 6:33; 1 Sam. 2:30). If we magnify our own name or our own deeds, we will sin, but if the Lord magnifies us, we can bring glory to His name (Josh. 3:7).

The Lord elected David (vv. 50-51). God's sovereign choice of David to be king, and His dynastic covenant with him, form the foundation for all that God did for His servant. Israel was called to be a witness to the nations, and it was David's responsibility to build a kingdom that would honor the name of the Lord. It's too bad that because of his sin with Bathsheba he brought reproach to God's name (2 Sam. 12:14). Nevertheless, David was God's king and God's anointed, and the covenant between God and David still stands and will ultimately be fulfilled in the reign of Jesus Christ in His kingdom.

Paul quoted verse 50 in Romans 15:9 as part of the wrap-up of his admonition to the believers in the churches in Rome that they receive one another and stop judging one another. The Gentile believers in Rome were enjoying their freedom in Christ, while many of the Jewish believers were still in bondage to the Law of Moses. Paul points out that Christ came to minister to both Jews and Gentiles by fulfilling God's promises to the Jews and dying for both Jews and Gentiles. From the very beginning of the nation, when God called Abraham and Sarah, the Lord had it in mind to include the Gentiles in His gracious plan of salvation (Gen. 12:1-3; Luke 2:29-32; John 4:22; Eph. 2:11ff).

The sequence in Romans 15:8-12 is significant. Jesus confirmed the promises made to Israel (v. 8), and Israel brought the message of salvation to the Gentiles (v. 9). Both believing Jews and Gentiles as one spiritual body now praise the Lord together (v. 10); and all the nations hear the good news of the Gospel (v. 11). When Jesus returns, He will reign over both Jews and Gentiles in His glorious kingdom (v. 12). From the very beginning, it was God's plan that the nation of Israel be His vehicle for bringing salvation to a lost world. "Salvation is of the Lord" (Jonah 2:9 NKJV) and "Salvation is of the Jews" (John 4:22 NKJV). The Gentiles owe a great debt to the Jews (Rom. 15:27), and Gentile Christians ought to pay that debt. They can show their appreciation to Israel by praying for their salvation (Rom. 9:1-5; 10:1) and for the peace of Jerusalem (Ps. 122:6), lovingly witnessing to them as God gives opportunity (Rom. 1:16), and sharing in their material needs (Rom. 15:27).

As you review this psalm, you can see what it was that thrilled the heart of David. He saw God and mentioned Him at least nineteen times. He saw God in the affairs of life, both the happy occasions and the storms that came. He saw God's purpose in his life and in the nation of Israel and rejoiced to be a part of it. But most exciting of all, in spite of the troubles David had experienced, he still saw the gentle hand of God, molding his life and accomplishing His purposes (v. 35). The enlarged troubles (Ps. 25:17) "enlarged" David (Ps. 4:1) and prepared him to take enlarged steps (2 Sam. 22:37 KJV) in the enlarged place God had prepared for him (22:20). That can be our experience as well.

TWELVE

David's Memories and Mistakes

The death of King David is not recorded in 2 Samuel, but in 1 Kings 2:1-12. However, 2 Samuel 23–24 record his last psalm, the names of his greatest soldiers, and the sad account of his sin of numbering the people. Chapters 21–24 serve as an "appendix" to 2 Samuel and seem to focus on the divine and human sides of leadership. A leader's decisions may have serious consequences, as proved by the sins of Saul (chap. 21) and David (chap. 24). Leaders must depend on the Lord and give Him the glory, as David's two psalms declare; and no leader can do the job alone, as indicated by the list of David's mighty men. Second Samuel 23–24 give us three portraits of David that illustrate the greatness and the humanness of this leader's life.

1. David the inspired singer (2 Sam. 23:1-7)

At least seventy-three of the psalms in the Book of Psalms are assigned to David, but his last one is found only here in 2 Samuel 23. The phrase "the last words of David" means "his last inspired written words from the Lord." The psalm may have been written during the closing days of his life, shortly before he died. Since the theme of the psalm is godly leadership, he may have written it especially for Solomon, but it has much to say to all of God's people today.

The privileges of leadership (vv. 1-2). David never ceased to marvel that God would call him to become the king of Israel, to lead God's people, fight God's battles, and even help to write God's Word. It was through David's descendants that God brought the Messiah into the world. From the human point of view, David was a "nobody," a shepherd, the youngest of eight sons in an ordinary Jewish family; nevertheless, God selected him and made him to become Israel's greatest king. The Lord had given David skillful hands and a heart of integrity (Ps. 78:70-72) and equipped him to know and do His will. As the son of Jesse, David was a member of the royal tribe of Judah, something that was not true of his predecessor Saul. (See Gen. 49:10.)

David didn't promote himself to achieve greatness; it was the Lord who chose him and elevated him to the throne (Deut. 17:15). The Lord spent thirty years training David, first with the sheep in the pastures, then with Saul in the army camp, and finally with his own fighting men in the Judean wilderness. Great leaders are trained in private before they go to work in public. "Talents are best nurtured in solitude," wrote Goethe; "character is best formed in the stormy billows of the world." David had both. He had been faithful in private as a servant, so God was able to elevate him publicly to be a ruler (Matt. 25:21). The Lord followed the same procedure when He prepared Moses, Joshua, Nehemiah, the apostles, and even His own Son (Phil. 2:5-11; Heb. 5:8). Dr. D. Martyn Lloyd-Jones used to say, "It is a tragic thing when a young man succeeds before he's ready for it." David was ready for the throne.

God empowers those whom He calls, and He anointed David with His Spirit (1 Sam. 16:12-13). Dr. A. W. Tozer said, "Never follow any leader until you see the oil on his forehead," which explains why so many gifted men came to David and joined his band. It takes more than talent and training to be an effective leader and to be able to recruit and train other leaders. Jesus reminded His disciples, and reminds us, "Without Me, you can do nothing" (John 15:5 NKJV). Religious leaders who follow the principles of what the world calls "success" rarely accomplish anything permanent that glorifies God. "He who does the will of God abides forever" (1 John 2:17 NKJV). It's good to be educated by men, but it's even more important to be trained by the Lord. "Our Lord was thirty years preparing for three years' service," wrote Oswald Chambers. "The modern stamp is three hours of preparation for thirty years of service."

But the Spirit not only empowered David for battle, He also inspired him to write beautiful psalms that still minister to our hearts. When you think of the trials that David had to endure in order to give us these psalms, it makes you appreciate them even more. David made it clear that he was writing the Word of God, not just religious poetry. Peter called David "a prophet" (Acts 2:30) and at Pentecost quoted what David wrote about the Messiah's resurrection and ascension (Acts 2:24-36). When you read the Psalms, you are reading the Word of God and learning about the Son of God.

The responsibilities of leadership (vv. 3-7). God didn't train David just to put him on display, but because He had important work for him to do; and so it is with every true leader. David was to rule over God's own people, "the sheep of his pasture" (Ps. 100:3), which is an awesome responsibility. It demands character and integrity ("just" = righteous) and a submissive attitude toward the Lord ("the fear of God"). Without righteousness and the fear of God, a leader becomes a dictator and abuses God's people, driving them like cattle instead of leading them like sheep. David was a ruler who served and a servant who ruled, and he had the welfare of his people on his heart (24:17). It encourages me today to see that even secular business specialists are comparing effective leaders to shepherds who care.[1]

David used a beautiful metaphor to picture the work of the leader: rain and sunshine that together produce useful fruit instead of painful thorns (vv. 4-7). David exemplified this principle in his own life, for when he came to the throne it meant the dawning of a new day for the nation of Israel. In this, he reminds us of what happened when Jesus came to earth (see Ps. 72:5-7; Isa. 9:2; 58:8, 60:1, 19; Mal. 4:1-3; Matt. 4:13-16; Luke 2:29-32). With the coronation of David, the storms that Saul had caused in the land were now over and the light of God's countenance was shining on His people. Under David's leadership, there would be a harvest of blessing from the Lord.

With God's help, leaders must create such a creative atmosphere that their colaborers will be able to grow and produce fruit. Ministry involves both sunshine and rain, bright days and cloudy days, but a godly leader's ministry will produce gentle rain that brings life and not storms that destroy. What a delight it is to follow a spiritual leader who brings out the best in us and helps us produce fruit for the glory of God! Unspiritual leaders produce thorns that irritate people and make progress very difficult (vv. 6-7).

But in his song, David went beyond the principles of leadership to celebrate the coming of Messiah (v. 5). David mentioned the covenant the Lord made with him (2 Sam. 7), a covenant that guaranteed him a dynasty forever and a throne forever, a covenant that was fulfilled in Jesus Christ (Luke 1:32-33, 68-79). The statements in verse 5 are best read as questions: "Is not my house right with God? Has he not made with me an everlasting covenant, arranged and secured in every part?" (NIV) The first question doesn't suggest that all of David's children were godly, for we know that they were not. It only declares that David's house (dynasty) was secure because of God's covenant promises. Nothing could change this covenant; it was everlastingly secured by the character of God.

In verse 5, David again used the image of fruit: "Will he not bring to fruition my salvation and grant me my every desire?" (NIV) David's desire was that God would fulfill His promise and send the Messiah, who would be born from David's descendants. The throne of Judah ended historically in 586 BC with the reign of Zedekiah, but that wasn't the end of David's family or the nation of Israel. The Lord providentially preserved Israel and David's seed so that Jesus Christ could be born in Bethlehem, the City of David. The nation was small and weak, but the Messiah came just the same! "A shoot will come up from the stump of Jesse; from his roots a Branch will bear fruit" (Isa. 11:1 NIV; see 4:2, 6:13, and 53:2). However, one day the evil people of the earth will be uprooted like thorns and burned (vv. 6-7; see Matt. 3:10, 12; 13:40-42).

2. David the gifted leader (2 Sam. 23:8-38; 1 Chron. 11:10-47)
Here are listed the names and some of the exploits of the leading men who followed David and stood with him during the difficult years of exile and during his reign.

The first "three mighty men" (vv. 8-12; 1 Chron. 11:10-14). Josheb-Basshebeth is named first; he was also known as Adino and Jashobeam (v. 8; 1 Chron. 11:11). He was chief of the captains in David's army and was famous for killing eight hundred enemy soldiers "at one time." First Chronicles 11:11 says he killed three hundred men. As we've already noted, the transmission of numbers from manuscript to manuscript by copyists sometimes led to these minor differences. Did the fear of the Lord drive all these men over a cliff, or did Jashobeam's courage inspire others to enter the battle and he got the credit for the victory? How he accomplished this feat isn't disclosed, but it's unlikely that he killed them one at a time with his spear.

Eleazar (vv. 9-10) was from the tribe of Benjamin (1 Chron. 8:4) and fought beside David against the Philistines, probably at Pas Dammim (1 Sam. 17:1; 1 Chron. 11:12-13). While many of the Israelite soldiers were retreating, he remained in his place and fought until the sword was "welded" to his hand. The Lord honored the faith and courage of David and Eleazar and gave Israel a great victory, after which the other soldiers returned to the field to strip the dead and claim the spoils. Like David, Eleazar wasn't selfish about sharing the spoils of battle because the victory had come from the Lord (1 Sam. 30:21-25).

The third "mighty man" was Shammah (vv. 11-12), who also was used of the Lord to bring victory at Pas Dammim (1 Chron. 11:13-14). But why risk your life to defend a field of lentils and barley? Because the land belonged to the Lord (Lev. 25:23) and was given to Israel to use for His glory (Lev. 18:24-30). Shammah didn't want the Philistines to control what belonged to Jehovah, for the Jews were stewards of God's land. To respect the land meant to honor the Lord and His covenant with Israel.

The second "three mighty men" (vv. 13-17; 1 Chron. 11:15-19). These three aren't named, but they were a part of the "thirty" listed in verses 24-29. This suggests that they were not the three men named previously. All people are created equal before God and the law, but all people are not equal in gifts and abilities; some people have greater gifts and opportunities than others. However, the fact that we can't achieve like "the first three" shouldn't keep us from doing less than our best and perhaps establishing a "second three." God doesn't measure us by what He helped others do but by what He wanted us to do with the abilities and opportunities He graciously gave us.

The fact that David was hiding in a cave near Bethlehem suggests that this event took place either during the time that David was fleeing from Saul or shortly after he was made king in Hebron and the Philistines attacked him (2 Sam. 5:17; 1 Chron. 14:8). It was harvest time, which meant there had been no rain and the cisterns were empty. No water was available in the cave, and David thirsted for the water from the well at Bethlehem that he used to drink from when he was a boy. The text suggests that David spoke to himself about the water and didn't issue any orders, but the three men wanted to please their leader more than anything else. They were close enough to hear his whispered words, loyal enough to take his wish as their command, and brave enough to obey at any cost. They traveled twelve miles, broke through enemy lines, and came back with the water. What an example for us to follow in our relationship with the Captain of our salvation!

No matter what the Lord put in David's hands, he used it to honor God and help God's people—a sling, a sword, a harp, a scepter, even a cup of water—and this occasion was no exception. When David looked into the cup, he didn't see water; he saw the blood of the three men who had risked their lives to satisfy his desire. To drink that water would demean all his men and cheapen the brave deed of the three heroes. It would communicate that their lives really weren't important to him. Instead, David turned the cave into a temple and poured the water out as a drink offering to the Lord, as he had seen the priests do at the tabernacle. The drink offering accompanied the giving of another sacrifice, such as the burnt offering, and was not offered independently. It was an act of dedication that symbolized a person's life poured out in the service of the Lord. The three men had given themselves as a sacrifice to the Lord to serve David (Rom. 12:1), so David added his offering to theirs to show them he was one with them in their devotion to Jehovah. To paraphrase his own words in 24:24, David would not treat as nothing that which had cost those three men everything. All leaders need to follow David's example and let their followers know how much they appreciate them and the sacrifices they make.

Jesus gave Himself as a sacrifice for us, and also as a drink offering (Ps. 22:14; Isa. 53:12). Paul used the image of the drink offering to describe his own dedication to the Lord (Phil. 2:17; 2 Tim. 4:6). Mother Teresa often said, "We can do no great things, only small things with great love." But doing small things because we love Christ turns them into great things. According to Jesus, whenever we show love and kindness to others and seek to meet their needs, we give Him a cup of cold water (Matt. 25:34-40).

Two special "mighty men" (vv. 18-23; 1 Chron. 11:20-25). Abishai (vv. 18-19) was David's nephew and the brother of Joab, the commander of David's army. He was also the brother of Asahel, who was slain treacherously by Abner; and Joab and Abishai killed Abner, much to David's regret (2 Sam. 2–3). Abishai was a courageous man who is commended here for killing three hundred enemy soldiers. However, sometimes he had more zeal than wisdom. While in Saul's camp with David one night, he wanted to kill King Saul, an offer that David rejected (1 Sam. 26); and he also offered to cut off Shimei's head because he cursed David (16:9-11; 19:21). He led the army in the siege of Rabbah (10:10-14) and saved David's life during a battle with a giant (21:15-17). Abishai was loyal to David during Absalom's rebellion and was in charge of a third of David's army (18:2, 12).[2] Abishai was also in charge of "the second three" and was held in high honor.

Benaiah (vv. 20-23; 1 Chron. 11:22-25) was a remarkable man who was born to serve as a priest (1 Chron. 27:5) but became a soldier and the commander of David's bodyguard (8:18; 20:23). In the Bible, there are priests who became prophets, such as Jeremiah, Ezekiel, and John the Baptist, but Benaiah is the only priest named who became a soldier. He performed valiantly on the battlefield and fought some interesting battles. F. W. Boreham has a wonderful sermon about Benaiah killing the lion in which he points out that Benaiah met the worst of enemies (a lion) in the worst of places (a pit) under the worst of conditions (on a snowy day) – and he won! Benaiah was loyal to the house of David and supported Solomon when he came to the throne (1 Kings 1:8-10). When Joab tried to make Adonijah king, it was Benaiah who executed him, thus fulfilling David's command to Solomon (1 Kings 2:5-6). Solomon made Benaiah the head of his army in Joab's place (1 Kings 2:35; 4:4; 1 Chron. 27:5-6). Benaiah's son Jehoiada didn't follow a military career but became a counselor to King Solomon, replacing Ahithophel (27:34).

The Thirty (vv. 24-39; 1 Chron. 11:26-47). Saul may have stood head and shoulders above everybody else, but it was David who had the kind of character and stature that attracted men who were looking for true leadership. One mark of real leaders is that they have devoted followers and not just self-seeking flatterers and parasites. (The official term is "sycophants," from a Greek word meaning "an informer." The American and English slang expression would be "bootlicker.") Saul's officers were men he couldn't trust and who had to be bribed into loyal service (see 1 Sam. 22:6ff), but David's men would have died for their leader, and some of them did.

Since ancient peoples often had two or more names that could have alternate spellings, it's not easy to correlate the list in 2 Samuel 23 with the one in 1 Chronicles 11. Some names on the

Samuel list are missing from the Chronicles list, but the latter list contains sixteen extra names (11:41-47). Perhaps they were replacements or alternates.[3] Those not mentioned in the Chronicles list are Shammah son of Agee (v. 11), Elika (v. 25), Eliam (v. 34), and Igal (v. 36). The differences between the two lists are minor and doubtless the composition of this group changed from time to time as men died and were replaced.

In this list, the men are divided into four groups: the three mighty men (vv. 8-12), the second three mighty men (vv. 13-17),[4] two special leaders (vv. 18-23), and "The Thirty" exceptional soldiers (vv. 24-39).[5] But does verser 36 record one man's name ("Igal the son of Nathan who was the son of Hagri") or the names of two men ("Igal the son of Nathan, and the son of Hagri")? Except for the three men who brought David the water, the names of all the other men are given, so it seems strange that one man's name would be omitted. It's likely that verse 36 registers the name of one man, which means there were thirty-two soldiers in "The Thirty"—the twenty-nine named on the list, plus the three unnamed men of verses 13-17. Perhaps the term "The Thirty" was simply a code name for David's elite soldiers, regardless of how many there were, just as "The Twelve" was a code name for the Lord's apostles. If you add to the thirty-two men the three mighty men of verses 8-12, plus Abishai and Benaiah, you have the total of thirty-seven given in verse 39.

Two names are familiar to us: Asahel, the nephew of David and brother of Joab and Abishai (v. 24), and Uriah the Hittite, the husband of Bathsheba (v. 39; 1 Chron. 11:41). Both of them were dead, but their names remained on the list of great warriors. How tragic that David took the life of one of his best soldiers just to cover up sin!

Two other facts are worth noting. First, David didn't do the job alone; he had the help of many devoted followers. We think of David as a mighty warrior, and he was, but how far would he have gotten without his loyal and gifted soldiers? Most of the men listed came from Judah. This is to be expected since Judah was David's tribe and he reigned there before the nation was united.

But "The Thirty" also included three men from Benjamin, the tribe of Saul, and several soldiers from neighboring nations. All these men recognized that God's hand was upon David and they wanted to be a part of what God was doing. The diversity of the commanders in his army speaks well of his leadership.

Second, God noted each man, had most of their names recorded in His Word, and will one day reward each one for the ministry he performed. David's name is mentioned over a thousand times in the Bible, while most of these men are mentioned but once or twice. However, when they meet the Lord, "then each one's praise will come from God" (1 Cor. 4:5 NKJV).

Joab was commander of the entire army (20:23), but he's mentioned in this military roster only in connection with his brothers Abishai (v. 18) and Asahel (v. 24; 1 Chron. 11:20, 26). In the end, Joab was disloyal to David and tried to put Adonijah on the throne, and this cost him his life (1 Kings 2:28-34).

3. David the repentant sinner (2 Sam. 24; 1 Chron. 21)

Second Samuel 24:1 states that God incited David to number the people, while 1 Chronicles 21:1 names Satan as the culprit. Both are true: God permitted Satan to tempt David in order to accomplish the purposes He had in mind. Satan certainly opposed God's people throughout all of Old Testament history, but this is one of four instances in the Old Testament where Satan is named specifically and seen openly at work. The other three are when he tempted Eve (Gen. 3), when he attacked Job (Job 1–2) and when he accused Joshua the high priest (Zech. 3).[6]

A proud king (vv. 1-9; 1 Chron. 21:1-6). There was nothing illegal about a national census, if it was done according to the rules laid down in Exodus 30:11-16 (and see Num. 3:40-51). The half shekel received at the census was used to pay the bills for the sanctuary of God (Ex. 38:25-28). As a good Jewish citizen, Jesus paid his temple tax (Matt. 17:24-27), even though He knew that much of the ministry at the temple in that day was corrupt and had been rejected by His Father (Matt. 23:37–24:1). The phrase "the people" used in 2 Samuel 24:2, 4, 9, 10 refers to the Jewish military forces and is used this way in the Authorized Version of 1 Samuel 4:3, 4, 17. But the census that David ordered wasn't to collect the annual temple tax; it was a military census to see how big his army was, as verse 9 makes clear. But there had been military censuses in Israel in the past and the Lord hadn't judged the nation (Num. 1 and 26). What was there about this census that was wrong?

Joab and his captains were against the project (v. 4) and Joab's speech in verse 3 suggests that David's command was motivated by pride. The king wanted to magnify his own achievements rather than glorify the Lord. David may have rationalized this desire by arguing that his son Solomon was a man of peace who had no military experience. David wanted to be certain that, after his death, Israel would have the forces needed to preserve the peace. Another factor may have been David's plan to organize the army, the government, and the priests and Levites so that Solomon could manage things more easily and be able to build the temple (1 Chron. 22–27).

Whatever the cause, the Lord was displeased (1 Chron. 21:7), but He permitted Joab and his captains to spend the next nine months and twenty days counting the Israelites twenty years old and upward who were fit for military service. Sometimes God's greatest judgment is simply to let us have our own way. The census takers left Jerusalem, traveled east across the Jordan, and started counting at Aroer in the vacinity of the Dead Sea. Then they moved north through Gad and Gilead to Israel's northernmost border, where David had conquered the territory and expanded his kingdom (2 Sam. 8). The men then went west to Tyre and Sidon and then south to Beersheba in Judah, Israel's farthest border city.

From Beersheba, they returned to Jerusalem, but they didn't count the Levites (who were exempted from military duty, Num. 1:49; 2:33) and the men of Benjamin. The tabernacle was located at Gibeon in Benjamin (1 Chron. 16:39-40; 21:29) and Joab may have thought it unwise to invade holy territory on such a sinful mission. Anyway, Saul had come from Benjamin and there may still have been pockets of resistance in the tribe. Benjamin was too close to home and Joab didn't want to take any chances. The incomplete total was 1,300,000 men.[7]

A convicted king (24:10-14; 1 Chron. 21:7-13). Realizing that he had been foolish in pursuing the project, David confessed his sin and sought the Lord's face. At least six times in Scripture we find David confessing "I have sinned" (2 Sam. 12:13; 24:10, 17; Ps. 41:4 and 51:4; 1 Chron. 21:8). When he confessed his sins of adultery and murder, David said, "I have sinned"; but when he confessed his sin of numbering the people, he said, "I have sinned *greatly*" (italics mine). Most of us would consider his sins relating to Bathsheba far worse than the sin of numbering the people, and far more foolish, but David saw the enormity of what he had done. David's sins with Bathsheba took the lives of four of David's sons (the baby, Amnon, Absalom, and Adonijah) plus the life of Uriah; but after the census, God sent a plague that took the lives of seventy thousand people. The Lord must have agreed with David that he had indeed sinned greatly.

David's sin with Bathsheba was a sin of the flesh, a yielding to lust after an afternoon of laziness (11:2; Gal. 5:19), but the census was a sin of the spirit (see 2 Cor. 7:1), a willful act of rebellion against God. It was motivated by pride, and pride is number one on the list of the sins that God hates (Prov. 6:16-17). "Pride is the ground in which all the other sins grow," wrote William Barclay, "and the parent from which all the other sins come." Both Scripture and civil law make a distinction between sudden sins of passion and willful sins of rebellion and treat the guilty parties differently (Deut. 19:1-13; Ex. 21:12-14). The census was willful rebellion, and David sinned against a flood of light. Furthermore, God gave David over nine months' time to repent, but he refused to yield. In the various scenes in David's history, Joab doesn't come across as a godly man, but even Joab was opposed to this project, and so were his officers. David should have heeded their counsel, but he was determined to have a census.

God in His grace forgives our sins when we confess them (1 John 1:9), but in His righteous government, He allows us to reap the consequences. In this case, the Lord even gave David the privilege of choosing the consequences. Why? Because David's disobedience was a sin of the will, a deliberate choice on David's part, so God allowed him to make another choice and name the punishment. Gad[8] gave the king three choices and told him to consider them, make a decision, and give his answer when the prophet returned.

Between the first and second visits, David must have sought the face of the Lord, for God lowered the famine period from seven years to three years, which explains the seeming discrepancy between 2 Samuel 24:13 and 1 Chronicles 21:12. In His mercy, God shortened the days of the suffering for His chosen people (Matt. 24:22). The three punishments are named in God's covenant with Israel (Deut. 28), so David shouldn't have been surprised: *famine—28:23-24, 38-40; military defeat—28:25-26, 41-48; pestilence—28:21-22, 27-28, 35, 60-60.*[9] In Jewish law, the unintentional sin of the high priest was equivalent to the sin of the entire congregation (Lev. 4:1-3, 13-14), so how much more would the penalties apply to a king who had sinned intentionally! Knowing the mercy of the Lord, David wisely chose pestilence for his punishment.

A repentant king (24:15-25; 1 Chron. 21:14-30). The plague started the next day at morning and continued for the appointed three days, with the judgment angel ending his work at Jerusalem, just as Joab and his men had done (v. 8). David's shepherd's heart was broken because of this judgment and he pleaded with the Lord to punish him instead. Why would God kill seventy thousand men and yet keep David alive? But we must note that 24:1 says that God was angry *with Israel* and not with David, so He must have been punishing the people for some sin they had committed. It's been suggested that this plague took the lives of the Israelites who had followed Absalom in his rebellion and didn't want David as their king. This may be so, but the text doesn't tell us.

God permitted David to see the judgment angel hovering over Jerusalem near the threshing floor of Araunah (Ornan), a

Jebusite. The Jebusites were the original inhabitants of Jerusalem, so Ornan had submitted to David's rule and become a reputable citizen of Jerusalem. We aren't told that David heard God's command to the angel to cease plaguing the people, but David knew that God was merciful and gracious, so he begged for mercy for "the sheep of his pasture' (Ps. 100:3). The elders of Israel were with David (1 Chron. 21:16) and with him fell to the ground in humble contrition and worship. It was David's sin that precipitated the crisis, but perhaps they realized that the nation had also sinned and deserved to feel God's rod of discipline.

Once again, the prophet Gad appeared on the scene, this time with a message of hope. David was to build an altar on Ornan's threshing floor and there offer sacrifices to the Lord, and the plague would cease. As king, David could have appropriated the property (1 Sam. 8:14) or even borrowed it, but he insisted on purchasing it. David knew the high cost of sinning and he refused to give the Lord something that had cost him nothing. For fifty shekels of silver he purchased the oxen for sacrifices and the wooden yokes for fuel, and for six hundred shekels of gold, he purchased the entire threshing floor (24:24; 1 Chron. 21:25). When the priest offered the sacrifices, God sent fire from heaven to consume them as a token of His acceptance (1 Chron. 21:26; Lev. 9:24).

Knowing that the king was well able to purchase his property, why was Ornan so anxious to give it to David absolutely free? Or was his offer just another instance of traditional Eastern courtesy in the art of bargaining? (See Gen. 23.) Perhaps Ornan remembered what happened to Saul's descendants because of what Saul did to the Gibeonites (21:1-14) and he didn't want the lives of his sons threatened (1 Chron. 21:20). The King James translation of verse 23 is a bit awkward and gives the idea that Ornan himself was a king, so the NIV or NASB should be consulted.

The land that David purchased was no ordinary piece of property, for it was the place where Abraham had put his son Isaac on the altar (Gen. 22) and where Solomon would build the temple (1 Chron. 22:1; 2 Chron. 3:1). After the plague had ceased,

David consecrated the site to the Lord (Lev. 27:20-21) and used it as a place of sacrifice and worship. The altar and tabernacle were at Gibeon, but David was permitted to worship at Jerusalem. The land was sanctified and would one day be the site of God's temple. David announced, "This is the house of the Lord God, and this is the altar of the burnt offering for Israel" (1 Chron. 22:1), and from that time began to get everything ready for Solomon to build the temple.

If you were asked to name David's two greatest sins, you would probably reply, "His adultery with Bathsheba and his numbering of the people," and you would be right. *But out of* those *two great sins, God built a temple!* Bathsheba gave birth to Solomon and God chose him to succeed David on the throne. On the property David purchased and on which he erected an altar, Solomon built the temple and dedicated it to the glory of God. What God did for David is certainly not an excuse for sin (Rom. 6:1-2), because David paid dearly for committing those sins. However, knowing what God did for David does encourage us to seek His face and trust His grace when we have disobeyed Him. "But where sin abounded, grace abounded much more" (Rom. 5:20). What a merciful God we serve!

THIRTEEN

1 CHRONICLES 22–29

David's Legacy

David "served his own generation by the will of God" (Acts 13:36 NKJV). When you serve your own generation faithfully, you also serve future generations. "He who does the will of God abides forever" (1 John 2:17 NKJV). The legacy of David enriched God's people Israel for centuries. Not only did David provide all that was needed for the building of the temple, he also wrote songs and designed musical instruments to be used in the worship services (23:5). Even more, it was through David's family that the Savior came into the world, "the Root and Offspring of David" (Rev. 22:16), so David still enriches the church today.

When we hear David's name, we may think first of Bathsheba and David's sins, but these chapters present David the builder, the man who risked his life to gather wealth for the building of a temple to the glory of God. He's a great example for believers of every age who want to make their lives count for Christ and leave behind their own legacy of spiritual blessing.

1. Spiritual motivation

Some Bible readers today might be tempted to scan these chapters, skip all the lists of names, and go on to read about the reign of Solomon in 2 Chronicles; but to do so would be a great mistake. Think of the encouragement and guidance these chapters must have given to the Jewish remnant that returned to Jerusalem after the Babylonian captivity. (See the books of Ezra, Nehemiah, Haggai, and Zechariah.) These courageous people had to rebuild the temple and organize its ministry, and reading these chapters would remind them that they were doing God's work. God gave each detail of the original temple and its ministry to David, who then gave it to Solomon. Those "lists of names" helped Zerubbabel and Joshua the high priest examine the credentials of those who wanted to serve in the temple (Ezra 2:59-64), and refuse those who were not qualified.

These chapters encouraged the Jews in their labors centuries ago, and they can encourage us today as we seek to build the church (Eph. 2:19-22). When you read 1 Corinthians 3:9-23 and compare it with 1 Chronicles 22, 28, and 29, you see parallels that ought to encourage us to build the church the way God's Word commands.[1] David knew that God's temple had to be built with gold, silver, and costly stones (22:14; 29:1-5), and Paul took these materials and applied them spiritually to the local church. They stand for the wisdom of God as found in the Word of God (Prov. 2:1-10; 3:13-15; 8:10-21). Wood, hay, and straw can be picked up on the surface, but if you want gold, silver, and jewels, *you have to dig for them*. We don't build the local church on clever human ideas or by imitating the world; we build by teaching and obeying the precious truths of the Word of God. (See 1 Cor. 3:18-20 for Paul's view of the wisdom of this world.)

Solomon didn't have to draw his own plans for the temple, because the Lord gave the plans to David (28:11-12). As we read the Word and pray, the Lord shows us His plans for each local church. "Work out your own salvation [Christian ministry] with fear and trembling" (Phil. 2:12-13 NKJV) was written to a congregation of believers in Philippi, and though it has personal application for all believers, the emphasis is primarily on the ministry of the congregation collectively. Some local church leaders run from one seminar to another, seeking to learn how to build the church, when they probably ought to stay home, call the church to prayer, and seek the mind of God in His Word. God has different plans for each church, and we're not supposed to blindly imitate each other.

The temple was built to display the glory of God, and our task in the local church is to glorify God (1 Cor. 10:31; 14:25). When Solomon dedicated the temple, God's glory moved in (1 Kings 8:6-11); but when Israel sinned, the glory moved out (Ezek. 10:4, 18-19; 11:22-23). We wonder how many local churches go through the motions of worship Sunday after Sunday, yet there's no evidence of the glory of God.

The temple was to be "a house of prayer for all nations" (Isa. 56:7), but the religious leaders in Jesus' day had made it into a den of thieves (Matt. 21:13; Lk.19:46; Jer. 7:11). A den of thieves is the place where thieves run to hide after they've done their wicked deeds, which suggests that a service in a local church can be a good place to go to pretend to be spiritual (1 John 1:5-10). How many local churches are known for their effective ministry of prayer? They may be houses of music, education, and even social activities, but are they houses of prayer?

The temple was built and God honored it with His presence because the leaders and people gave their best to the Lord, sacrificed, and followed His directions. This is a good example for us to follow today. We are privileged to assist in the building of the church, and our motive must be only the glory of God.

2. Careful preparation (1 Chron. 22:1-19)

The Lord didn't permit David to build the temple, but He did honor the preparation David made for his son Solomon to do the job. "Well begun is half done" says the old proverb, and David was careful to have Solomon, the people and the materials prepared for the great project. (See vv. 3, 5 and 14.)

The site, materials and workers (vv. 1-4). We're not sure when the Lord began to give David the plans for the temple and its personnel, but the purchase of Ornan's property seemed to be the signal for action. When God sent fire from heaven to consume

David's offerings (21:26), David knew that his sin was forgiven and that he was back in fellowship with the Lord. But David also perceived that his altar was now very special to the Lord and he continued to sacrifice there instead of going to the tabernacle at Gibeon. The Lord let him know that Mount Moriah was the place where He wanted the temple to be built. It's possible that David wrote Psalm 30 at this time, even though as yet there was no actual building to dedicate. By faith, he dedicated to the Lord the property he had purchased and the building that would one day stand on it.[2]

David enlisted both Jews and resident aliens (1 Kings 5:13-18) to help construct the temple. This division of David's government was under Adoram (2 Sam. 20:24), also called Adoniram (1 Kings 4:6).[3] The 30,000 Jewish workers cut timber in Lebanon for a month and then returned home for two months, while the 150,000 "alien" laborers cut and delivered massive stones from the hills, supervised by Jewish foremen (1 Kings 5:13-18, and see 9:15-19; 2 Chron. 2:17-18). The fact that Gentiles worked along with the Jews suggests that the temple was indeed a house for all nations. We must not think that these resident aliens were treated as slaves, because the Law of Moses clearly prohibited such practices (Ex. 22:21; 23:9; Lev. 19:33).

For years, David had been amassing the materials for the temple, the total value of which was beyond calculation. Much of it came from the spoils of the battles David had fought and won (18:9-11; 26:26-28). David the warrior had defeated Israel's enemies and taken their wealth so that Solomon his son would have the peace and provisions necessary to build the house of God.

Solomon the builder (vv. 5-16). Some biblical chronologists believe David was about sixty years old when he inaugurated the temple building program, but we don't know how old Solomon was. David said his son was "young and inexperienced" (22:5; 29:1 NIV), and after his accession to the throne, Solomon called himself "a little child" (1 Kings 3:7). This explains why David admonished and encouraged his son several times to obey the Lord and finish the work God had assigned to him (22:6-16;

28:9-10, 20-21). David also admonished the leaders to encourage and assist their new king in this great project. David wanted everything to be prepared before his own death so that Solomon would have everything he needed to build the house of God.

David encouraged Solomon by assuring him that the temple project was the will of God; therefore, the Lord would help him finish it (vv. 6-10). God had enabled his father to fight the Lord's battles and bring about peace for Israel, and now it was time to build God's house (2 Sam. 7:9). The Lord had told David that a son would be born to him to accomplish this task (7:12-16; 1 Chron. 17:11; see Deut. 12:8-14). The emphasis David made was that the temple was to be built, not for the glory of the name of David or even of Solomon, but the name of the Lord (vv. 7, 8, 10, 19). David wanted to be sure that Solomon would honor the Lord and not build a monument to honor himself.

David further encouraged his son by reminding him of the faithfulness of God (vv. 11-13). If he would trust the Lord and obey Him fully, the Lord would maintain the peace and security of Israel and enable him to complete the project (see 28:7-9, 20). The words "Be strong, and of good courage; dread not, nor be dismayed" remind us of how Moses encouraged Joshua his successor (Deut. 31:5-8, 23); the Lord repeated that encouragement after Moses died (Josh. 1:6, 9). Moses and Joshua were faithful men, and God saw them through all their trials and enabled them to complete their work. He would do the same for Solomon.

The third encouragement David gave his son was the great amount of wealth the king had accumulated for the project, along with the large number of workers who were conscripted (vv. 14-16). It seems incredible, but the king said he had amassed 3,750 tons of gold and 37,500 tons of silver, and that there was so much bronze and iron that it couldn't be weighed. At least Solomon wouldn't have to take up any collections!

The leaders of Israel (vv. 17-19). David ordered the leaders to cooperate with Solomon and help him complete the project. He reminded them that the peace and rest they enjoyed was only because God had used David to defeat Israel's foes and expand her borders. (Note the mention of "rest" in vv. 9 and 18 and in 23:25.) But the temple was for the Lord, so it was imperative that the leaders seek Him and have their hearts right before Him. David had his throne in Jerusalem and he wanted the ark—the throne of God—to be there also. His only concern was that the name of the Lord be glorified.

3. Temple organization (1 Chron. 23:1–27:34)

David knew that the ministers of the temple also had to be organized and prepared if God was to be glorified. Too often local church building programs concentrate so much on the financial and the material that they ignore the spiritual, and then a backslidden and divided congregation meets to dedicate the new edifice! A gifted administrator, David organized the Levites (chap. 23), the priests (chap. 24), the temple singers (chap. 25), and the temple officers (chap. 26). David wanted to be sure that everything in God's house would be done "decently and in order" (1 Cor. 14:40 NKJV). In making these decisions, David and his two priests drew lots (24:5-6, 31; 25:8; 26:13-14, 16). This was the process Joshua used when he gave the tribes their inheritance in the Promised Land (Josh. 14:2; 23:4).

But organization wasn't an end in itself, for these people were being organized for service. The phrase "for the service of the house of the Lord" (or its equivalent) is used several times in these chapters to remind us that ministry is the major responsibility of God's servants in God's house. (See 23:24, 26, 28, 32; 25:1, 6, 8, 30; 28:13, 14, 20, 21; 29:5, 7; 2 Chron. 31: 16, 17.) It's one thing to fill an office, but quite something else to use that office to serve the Lord and His people.

The Levites (23:1-32; see also chap. 6). The author of Chronicles doesn't record the family struggle that occurred when Solomon became king (1 Kings 1–2), but verse 1 indicates an earlier appointment and 29:22 a second one. However, verse 1 may simply mean that David announced Solomon as his successor, as in 28:4-5, while 29:22 describes the actual coronation. (We get the impression that Solomon's coronation described in

1 Kings 1 was very hastily arranged.) Solomon's formal public accession to the throne is described in 29:21-25.

The Levites assisted the priests in the sanctuary ministry and were required by the law to be at least thirty years old (v. 3; Num. 4:3; see also Num. 8:24). Later that was lowered to twenty years (v. 24). The 38,000 Levites were divided into four groups, each with a specific ministry: 24,000 Levites who helped the priests in the sanctuary, 6,000 who were "officers and judges" (see 26:1-32), 4,000 who were gatekeepers ("porters" KJV; see 26:1-19), and 4,000 who were singers (see 25:1-31). There was one temple, one high priest, one divine law, and one Lord to serve, but there was a diversity of gifts and ministries, not unlike the church today. The fact that the Levites took care of the sanctuary while the priests served at the altar didn't mean that their work was less important to the ministry or to the Lord. Each servant was important to Lord and each ministry was necessary.

David not only organized the sanctuary musicians, but he also provided them with proper musical instruments to use in praising the Lord (v. 5; 2 Chron. 29:25-27; Amos 6:5). Nothing that the priests and Levites did in the temple was left to chance or human invention, but was ordained by the Lord. Nadab and Abihu, the sons of Aaron the first high priest (24:1-2), were killed by the Lord for devising their own form of worship (Lev. 10).

The Levitical duties are given in verses 24-32. The Israelites were at rest in their land and no longer a nomadic people, so the Levites didn't have to carry the various parts of the tabernacle from place to place (see Num. 4). The construction of the temple meant that the Levites would need new assignments. One of their tasks would be to keep the temple clean and in good repair and make sure that the temple precincts were ceremonially pure. They also saw to it that the supply of meal was available for the offerings. Whenever the daily, monthly, and annual sacrifices were offered, the Levite choir would provide praise to the Lord.

The priests (24:1-31). It was important that the priests truly be descendants of Aaron. In David's day, he had two high priests, Zadok, a descendant of Aaron through Eleazar, and Ahimelech, the son of Abiathar, who was from the line of Ithamar. Abiathar was David's friend and priest during his exile days (1 Sam. 20:20ff) and also during the rebellion of Absalom (2 Sam. 15:24-29). Unfortunately, Abiathar wasn't loyal to Solomon and sided with Adonijah in his quest for the throne, and Solomon had to banish him from Jerusalem (1 Kings 2:22-27). Abiathar came from the line of Eli, and that line was rejected and judged by God (1 Sam. 2:30-33; also see 2 Sam. 22:26-27). The twenty-four families (clans) of priests were assigned by lot to serve in the sanctuary at scheduled times and the rest of the time would be in the priestly cities instructing the people. This procedure was still being followed when Zacharias served in the temple (Luke 1:5-9). He was from the clan of Abijah (24:10).

The musicians (25:1-31). Apart from the ritual blowing of the trumpets (Num. 10), nowhere in the Law of Moses is there any mention of music in connection with Jewish worship, yet this chapter describes an elaborate organization of twenty-four courses of singers and musicians. David was a writer of psalms and a gifted musician (2 Sam. 23:1-2; 1 Sam. 16:18) and it's likely that the sanctuary musical worship came to fruition under his direction (v. 6), and the Lord approved these innovations (2 Chron. 29:25). Harps, lyres, and cymbals are mentioned here (v. 1), and trumpets are mentioned elsewhere (1 Chron. 13:8; 15:24, 28; 2 Chron. 5:13; 20:28). There were also choirs (1 Chron. 15:27).

Three gifted Levites were put in charge of the instrumental music and the singing in the worship services. Asaph wrote at least twelve psalms (50, 73–83) and played the cymbals (16:5). Heman was also called "the king's seer" (v. 5), which suggests that he had a special gift of discerning the Lord's will. The Lord promised to give Heman a large family (v. 5 NIV), and all his children were musicians. Jeduthun's name is related to "Judah" and means "praise," a good name for a choir director. Jeduthun is also associated with Psalms 39, 62 and 77.

The word "prophesy" is used three times in verses 1-3 to describe the ministry of Asaph, Heman, and Jeduthun. The word usually refers to the ministry of the prophets in declaring God's

Word. As has often been said, "The prophets were *forth*-tellers as well as *fore*-tellers." They spoke to present needs and didn't just predict future events. Miriam led the women in praising the Lord, and she was called a prophetess (Ex. 15:20). The root of the Hebrew word *naba* means "to bubble, to boil up," referring to the fervor and excitement of the prophet declaring God's message. Others say it comes from an Arabic root that means "to announce." The point is that the men who led Israel's sanctuary worship were not necessarily prophets in the technical sense, but they and their singers declared the Word (God's message) with enthusiasm and joy.

Temple officers (26:1-32). These officials included gatekeepers (vv. 1-19), treasurers (vv. 20-28), and miscellaneous officials scattered outside Jerusalem (vv. 29-32). The gatekeepers were assigned to guard the temple gates, with four guards at the north and south gates and six at the east and west gates (vv. 17-18 NLT). Two guards watched over the storehouse, and there were also guards outside the temple area. There are details about the temple area that aren't recorded in Scripture, and this makes it difficult for us to be exact in our description. It seems that the gatekeepers watched the people come and go and made sure that nobody was deliberately defiling the temple or behaving in a way that disgraced the sanctuary of the Lord.

The treasurers (vv. 20-28) guarded the two temple treasuries, one for general offerings and the other for "dedicated things" from the people, especially the spoils of war (vv. 20-28). (See 2 Kings 12:4-16.) Saul and David added to this treasury, but so did other leaders, such as Samuel the prophet and Abner and Joab, the two generals.

The third group of temple officers (vv. 29-32) were the "officers and judges" assigned to tasks away from the temple and even west of the Jordan. They kept the king in touch with the affairs of the tribes of Reuben and Gad and the half tribe of Manasseh. But these officers were also responsible to keep these tribes involved in "every matter pertaining to God" (v. 32 NIV), that is, the all-important religious events of the nation. Separated from the other tribes, the trans-Jordanic Israelites might easily grow careless about observing the annual feasts or even the weekly Sabbaths. This explains why these officers are listed among the temple workers. It's also likely that these officers were also responsible to collect taxes.

4. Military administration (1 Chron. 27:1-34)

For Solomon to be able to build the temple, Israel had to remain a strong nation, at peace with her neighbors, for young Solomon wasn't a military genius like his father David. It was necessary to organize the army, the tribal leaders, and the managers and counselors who served the king personally.

The captains (vv. 1-15). David's army consisted of 288,000 men—not an excessively large standing army—made up of twelve divisions of 24,000 each, so that each man served one month out of the year. However, if a military emergency arose, the entire army could be called up. Each monthly military division was in charge of one of David's "mighty men," who are listed in 1 Chronicles 11. The twelve commanders are: Jashobeam (vv. 2-3; see 11:11); Dodai (v. 4; see 11:12); Benaiah, head of David's personal bodyguard (vv. 5-6; see 11:22-25); Asahel, David's nephew (v. 7; see 11:26); Shamhuth (v. 8; see 11:27); Ira (v. 9; see 11:28); Helez (v. 10; see 11:27); Sibbecai (v. 11; see 11:29); Abiezer (v. 12; see 11:28); Maharai (v. 13; see 11:30); another Benaiah (v. 14; see 11:31); and Heldai (v. 15; see 11:30).

The tribal leaders (vv. 16-24). Each of the tribes had a leader (Num. 1–2, 4) and the tribes were broken down into smaller units (tens, fifties, hundreds, thousands; Ex. 18:17-23), each unit with a leader. For some reason, Gad and Asher are not mentioned in this list, but to reach the number twelve, Levi is included along with both tribes of Joseph (Ephraim and Manasseh). The king could summon twelve men and through them eventually get the ear of all the people.

The mention of the tribes and their leaders brought to mind David's ill-fated census (21:1-17; 2 Sam. 24). This extra piece of information helps us understand why the numbers differ in the two accounts (24:9; 21:5), because Joab didn't finish the census and not all the numbers were recorded.

The king's managers (vv. 25-31). During Saul's reign, there was some kind of tax structure (1 Sam. 17:25), but this is not mentioned in the records of David's reign. Under Solomon, the taxes became intolerable (1 Kings 4:7, 26-28;12:1-24). David owned royal farms, orchards, vineyards, flocks, and herds, and from these he met the needs of the palace personnel. David had storehouses for his produce, and since his tastes weren't as expensive as Solomon's, what David received from the Lord went much further.

The king's counselors (vv. 32-34). Every leader needs an inner circle of counselors who will advise him, force him to examine his own decisions and motives, and help him seek the mind of the Lord. Jonathan, David's uncle, is given high recommendations. Jehiel appears to have been tutor to the sons in the royal family. Ahithophel had been David's trusted friend and wise adviser, but he sided with Absalom in the rebellion and committed suicide when Absalom rejected his counsel (2 Sam. 15:30-31; 16:15–17:23). Hushai was the man whose counsel was accepted by Absalom, which led to the downfall of the rebel army. Ahithophel's replacement was "Jehoiada son of Benaiah." This Benaiah is probably the son of David's trusted head of the royal bodyguard, Benaiah the priest. Abiathar the priest was one of David's must trusted helpers (1 Sam. 22:20-23), and though Joab and David were not intimates, David needed the head of his army in his inner circle if only to know what he was thinking. Joab didn't always have David's interests at heart.

5. Sincere consecration (1 Chron. 28:1–29:20)

No amount of human machinery and organization can take the place of heartfelt consecration to the Lord. David was going to leave the scene, an inexperienced son would follow him, and the construction of the temple was a task beyond any one man or group of men. Apart from the blessing of the Lord, the people could not hope to succeed. Leaders come and go, but the Lord remains; and it is the Lord whom we must please.

David challenges the leaders (28:1-8). David assembled at Jerusalem the leaders mentioned in the previous chapters and reviewed for them the story of his great desire to build a temple for the Lord. It's good for people to know the heart of their leader and how God has worked in his or her heart. He emphasized that it was the Lord who chose and anointed him and who chose Solomon to be his successor. He reminded the leaders of God's gracious covenant with the house of David and of their responsibility to obey the law of the Lord. If they kept the terms of the covenant and obeyed God, He would keep His promises and bless the nation. As long as they obeyed the terms of God's covenant, they would possess the land and enjoy its blessings.

David charges Solomon (28:9-10). Solomon had a great responsibility to set the example and obey the law of the Lord. A "perfect heart" means a heart wholly dedicated to the Lord, one that's not divided. It's unfortunate that in his later years Solomon became a double-minded man and began to worship idols, for this led to God's discipline and the division of the kingdom. For the second time, David admonished Solomon to "be strong" (22:13), and he would do it a third time before he finished his speech (v. 20). Dr. Lee Roberson has often said, "Everything rises and falls with leadership." If leadership is faithful to the Lord and trusting in Him, God will give success.

David conveys his gifts for the project (vv. 11-21). David's first gift to Solomon was a written plan for the temple and its furnishings (vv. 11-19). While the temple followed the pattern of the tabernacle in a general way, what Solomon built was larger and much more elaborate than what Moses built. David reminded Solomon that these plans were not suggestions from the Lord; they were a divine commission. The organization of the priests and Levites was also commanded by the Lord. Moses had to make everything according to the pattern God gave him on the mount (Ex. 25:9, 40; Heb. 8:5), and so did Solomon. The plans for the temple spelled out how much material should go into each piece of furniture and each part of the building (vv. 13-19), and nothing was to be changed.

David's second gift was another word of encouragement to strengthen Solomon's will and his faith (v. 20). Like Moses encouraging Joshua (Deut. 31:6-7), David told Solomon that the Lord would never forsake him and that he could find in God all the wisdom and strength he needed to complete the project.[5]

The third gift Solomon received from his father was a people prepared to work with him and complete the project (v. 21). We've seen how David organized the various levels of leaders, both civil and religious, so they could work harmoniously and follow their new king. Just as the Lord provided skillful people to construct the tabernacle (Ex. 35:25-35; 36:1-2), so He would provide the workers that Solomon needed to build the temple of Jehovah. This promise was fulfilled (2 Chron. 2:13-14). Furthermore, all the people would listen to their new king's commands and obey him.

David's fourth gift was his own store of wealth that he had accumulated for the building of the temple (29:1-5). According to 22:14, the spoils of battle devoted to the Lord amounted to 3,750 tons of gold and 37,500 tons of silver. David added from his own wealth 110 tons of gold and 260 tons of silver (v. 4). This means that David was responsible for providing 3,860 tons of gold and 37,760 tons of silver. But the king then urged his leaders to give generously to the "building fund" (vv. 6-9), and they contributed 190 tons of gold, plus another 185 pounds, 375 tons of silver, 675 tons of bronze, and 3,750 tons of iron, as well as precious stones. This sounds like Paul's "gold, silver, and precious stones" (1 Cor. 3:12). The remarkable thing about the leaders and their offering is that they gave willingly and "rejoiced with great joy" at the privilege! This time we're reminded of Paul's words in 2 Corinthians 8:1-5 and 9:7.

David calls on the Lord (29:10-21). This magnificent prayer begins with praise and adoration to the Lord (vv. 10-14). God had blessed David richly, so he blesses God thankfully! His words are a short course in theology. He blesses the God of Israel and acknowledges His greatness, power, glory, victory, and majesty. God owns everything! God is sovereign over all! His name is great and glorious! But who are David and his people that they should be able to give so lavishly to the Lord? After all, everything comes from Him, and when we give, we only return to the Lord that which He has graciously already given to us.

In contrast to the eternal God, David declares that he—the king!—is like any other human, an alien and a stranger on the earth. God is eternal, but human life is brief and nobody can prevent the inevitable hour of death. (Here David sounds like Moses in Ps. 90.) Since all things come from God, and life is brief, the wisest thing we can do is give back to God what He gives to us and make an investment in the eternal.

He assures the Lord that the offerings came from his heart and the hearts of his people, and that they gave joyfully and with sincerity. David prays that his people might always have hearts of generosity, gratitude, and joy, and that they might always be loyal to their God. In other words, may they worship God alone and not make wealth their God.

Like any godly father, David closed his prayer by interceding for his son Solomon, that he would always be obedient to what was written in the law, and that he might succeed in building the temple to the glory of God. ("Palace" in v. 19 KJV means "any large palatial structure.") He then called on the congregation to bless the Lord, and they obeyed and bowed low and even fell on their faces in submission and adoration. What a way to begin a building program!

6. Joyful celebration (1 Chron. 29:21-25)
The next day, David provided sacrifices for the Lord and a feast for his leaders. The burnt offerings were sacrificed to express the people's total dedication to the Lord. But David also offered fellowship offerings, and a part of each sacrifice was used for a fellowship meal. It was a joyful occasion that climaxed with the coronation of Solomon. It was very important that the representatives of all Israel agree that Solomon was God's appointed king; otherwise, he could never have led them in the building of the temple. David was anointed privately by Samuel (1 Sam. 16:13)

and publicly at Hebron on two occasions (2 Sam. 2:4; 5:3), so he was anointed three times. At the same celebration, Zadok was anointed high priest, which suggests that Abiathar was set aside. Eventually Abiathar turned traitor and supported Adonijah and was sent into retirement (1 Kings 2:26-27, 35).

The book closes on a sober note as it records the death of King David. A Russian proverb says, "Even the greatest king must at last be put to bed with a shovel." True, but some bring glory to God even from the grave! From that day on, the Jewish kings were all measured against David (1 Kings 3:3; 15:5; 2 Kings 18:3; 22:2; 14:3; 15:3, 34; 16:2; 18:3; 20:3).

David's legacy is a long one and a rich one. He unified the nation, gave the people peace in their land, and extended the borders of the kingdom. God chose him to establish the dynasty that eventually brought Jesus the Savior into the world. He provided much of the wealth that was used to build the temple, and the king who constructed it. He also purchased the site on which the temple would be built. God gave David the plans for the temple, and David recruited the workers to build it.

David wrote songs for the Levites to sing as they worshiped God, and he also provided the musical instruments. He organized the temple ministry and taught the people that the worship of God was the number-one priority for them and the nation. Before he died, he encouraged Solomon, challenged the leaders, and gave to the new king a united people, enthusiastic about building the house of God. We today learn from David's life both what to do and what to avoid. We read and meditate on David's hymns, and sometimes we sing them.

NOTES

Chapter 1

1. It's interesting that 1 Samuel records the scene of a messenger bringing bad news of defeat to Eli the priest (1 Sam. 4), and here a similar messenger brings what he thought was good news to David the king. Eli keeled over and died, but here the messenger was slain. In 1 Samuel, the ark was taken by the enemy, but later recovered by Israel; here the bodies of the royal family were taken and later recovered and buried.

2. Saul's death reminds us of Revelation 3:11: "Behold, I am coming quickly! Hold fast what you have, that no one may take your crown" (NKJV).

3. King Saul's namesake, Saul of Tarsus, began his ministry by falling (Acts 9:4; 22:7; 26:14), but at the end of his life, we see him standing boldly with his Lord (2 Tim. 4:16-17).

4. The KJV gives the impression that David wrote this song to encourage young men to learn how to use the bow, but the Hebrew text doesn't support this. The elegy was called "The Song of the Bow" possibly because of the reference to Jonathan's bow in verse 22. The name identified the tune that was used to sing the song. Certainly David wasn't encouraging the archers to practice more because Saul and Jonathan lost the battle, because his song extols their military prowess.

5. The Hebrew word translated "glory" can also be translated "gazelle." David saw Saul as a majestic deer that had been slain on the mountain.

6. "The sword devours" (i.e., eats, drinks) is a familiar metaphor in the Old Testament (Deut. 32:42; 2 Sam. 2:26; 11:25; Isa. 31:8; Jer. 12:12). Saul's sword devoured much blood and was satisfied.

7. It appears that the tribe of Judah, while cooperating with Saul and the other tribes, had been maintaining somewhat of a "separated" posture in those days (see 1 Sam. 11:8; 15:4; 17:52; 18:16; 30:26).

8. David was anointed three times: first privately by Samuel (1 Sam. 16:13), then publicly by the elders and people of Judah (2 Sam. 2:4),

and finally publicly by the whole nation (5:3).

Chapter 2

1. The name "baal" also belonged to Saul's granduncle (1 Chron. 9:36), and Jonathan's lame son Mephibosheth was also called "Merib-Baal" (1 Chron. 8:34).

2. Joab was David's nephew, but David didn't seem to have much control over him (see 3:39 and 18:5, 14.) At the end of David's reign, Joab conspired to make David's son Adonijah the next king; when Solomon took the throne, he had Joab executed for treason (1 Kings 2).

3. According to 2 Samuel 17:25, Zeruiah was either David's half sister or step sister. If Nahash was the mother of Abigail and Zeruiah, then she was Jesse's second wife. If Nahash was the father, then he sired Abigail and Zeruiah, died, and his unidentified wife married Jesse. Whoever she was, Zeruiah certainly was the mother of three remarkable men.

4. First Chronicles 27:7 tells us that Asahel's son Zebadiah succeeded his father as commander of his division.

5. There's an interesting pattern in 2 Samuel in which you find a list of names (children or officials) at the end of historical sections: 1:1–3:5; 3:6–5:16; 5:17–8:18; 9:1–20:26.

6. The situation reminds us of the Parable of the Prodigal Son (Luke 15:11-32). Abner, the "prodigal soldier," was coming home, and David gave him a banquet. Joab, the faithful "elder brother," might say to David, "I've been faithful to you and risked my life, and yet you never gave me a banquet!"

Chapter 3

1. How could this many people converge on Hebron and eat and drink for three days without upsetting the town and its economy? Where would all the food come from? First Chronicles 13:1 may give us the answer. While the chronicler gives us the totals of the military units loyal to David, perhaps only the officers of these military units attended the coronation, a total of about 3,750 men. Not every soldier was present, but every soldier was represented and through his officer gave his allegiance to the new king.

2. The name "Eliphelet" is found twice in the list and is also given as "Elpelet."

3. If the brave deed of the three mighty men occurred at this time, then David was in the Cave of Adullam (2 Sam. 23:13).

4. Some Old Testament scholars put this event later in David's career, after David's sin with Bathsheba and his numerous battles against his enemies (2 Sam. 8–12). See A Harmony of the Books of Samuel, Kings and Chronicles by William Day Crockett (Baker Book House, 1964).

5. It's not likely that these sacrifices were offered after every six steps as the procession moved toward Jerusalem. That would have made for a very long journey and would have required a great number of sacrifices. Once David was sure of God's approval, they marched on with confidence.

Chapter 4

1. The word "covenant" isn't used in 2 Samuel 7 but David used it in 23:5 when referring to the revelation given to him through Nathan.

2. Most scholars have concluded that Bathshua and Bathsheba were the same person. It was not unusual for a person in the ancient world to have more than one name or the name have more than one spelling.

3. First Chronicles 22:8 and 28:1-3 inform us that the fact that David shed much blood was another reason why God chose Solomon to build the temple.

4. In His covenant with Abraham, God promised him many descendents and later compared their number to the dust of the earth (Gen. 13:16) and the stars of the heaven (Gen. 15:1-6), suggesting an earthly people and a heavenly people. The Jews are God's earthly people and are promised an earthly kingdom, but all who trust Christ are of the seed of Abraham (Gal. 3:1-18) because all of us are saved by faith, not by obeying a law.

5. This is the third of four "official lists" found in 2 Samuel, and each one closes a major division of the book: 1:1–3:5 (David's sons in Hebron); 3:6–5:16 (David's sons in Jerusalem); 5:17–8:18 (David's officers in Jerusalem); and 9:1–20:26 (David's officers later in his reign).

6. One school of interpreters feels that David was only putting

Mephibosheth under "house arrest" to make certain that he didn't create any problems in the kingdom. Subsequent events proved that it was Ziba the manager who needed to be watched! And how much damage could a crippled young man do to Israel's greatest king? David brought Mephibosheth to his palace table, not to protect himself but to show his love to him for his father's sake.

7. "Kindness" (mercy) is sometimes connected with the making of a covenant. (See Deut. 7:9, 12; Josh. 2:12; 1 Sam. 20:8, 14-17; Dan. 9:4.)

8. Keep in mind that 2 Samuel wasn't written in chronological order, and verses like 8:12 are summaries of wars that the writer describes later.

9. In a prior battle, David was nearly killed by a giant named Ishbi-benob, and his nephew Abishai rescued him. At that time, the military leaders told David not to go to go to war anymore (2 Sam. 21:15-17), and he complied. His appearance at the Syrian campaign (10:15-19) was to take charge of troop movements but not to engage in hand-to-hand combat.

Chapter 5

1. There is no account of David's great sins found in 1 Chronicles. The book was written from the viewpoint of the priesthood; the emphasis is on the greatness of the kings, not their sins. David and Solomon are described as "ideal rulers."

2. Isaac Watts, "Divine Songs for Children" (1715).

3. The word "sent" is repeated often in chapters 11 and 12. See 11:1, 3, 4, 5, 6 (twice), 8, 12, 14, 18, 22; 12:1, 25, 27. David's sins kept a lot of people on the move!

4. *Professor Blaiklock's Handbook of Bible People*, by E. M. Blaiklock (London: Scripture Union, 1979), p. 210.

5. Joseph Butler, *Fifteen Sermons* (Charlottesville, VA: Ibis Publishing, 1987), p. 114

6. Saul used the words "I have sinned" three times, but didn't mean them (1 Sam. 15:24, 30; 26:21). David said "I have sinned" at least five times (2 Sam. 12:13; 24:10, 17 [1 Chron. 21:8, 17]; Pss. 41:4; 51:4). David was the Prodigal Son of the Old Testament, who repented and "came home" to find forgiveness (Luke 15:18, 21). For others who used

these words see Exodus 9:27; Numbers 22:34; Joshua 7:20; 2 Samuel 19:20; Matthew 27:4.

7. As with Jonah and the city of Nineveh, God's decree of judgment can be interrupted by the repentance of the people involved. (Nineveh didn't fall until over a century later.) The prediction that Bathsheba's baby would die was fulfilled that week because God chose to act at that time. God's character and purposes don't change, but He does change His timing and His methods to accomplish His purposes.

8. Since Scripture gives no definitive revelation on the subject of infant salvation, theologians have wrestled with the problem and good and godly believers disagree. For a balanced and compassionate theological study, see *When a Baby Dies* by Ronald H. Nash (Zondervan, 1999).

Chapter 6

1. Even after his death, Absalom's name and memory reminded people of evil (2 Sam. 20:6; 1 Kings 2:7, 28; 15:2, 10; 2 Chron. 11:20-21).

2. It's likely that David's second son, Kileab (or Daniel), died young, for apart from the royal genealogy, he is not mentioned in the biblical account (1 Chron. 3:1). \

3. Perhaps she was thinking of Abraham and Sarah (Gen. 20:12), but that was before the Law of Moses.

4. When Dinah was raped (Gen. 34), it was her full brothers Simeon and Levi who avenged her (see Gen. 29:32-35; 30:17-21.)

5. The Hebrew for "Amnon" is a diminutive form: "Has that little Amnon been with you?" Absalom didn't hide his utter dislike for his half brother. \

6. Did anybody know that Solomon was God's choice for the next king? Perhaps not, for the Lord hadn't revealed it. According to some chronologists, Solomon's birth occurred before Amnon's sin against Tamar, but Bathsheba had given birth to three other sons before she gave birth to Solomon (2 Sam. 5:14; 1 Chron. 3:5; 14:4). God promised David that one of his sons would succeed him and build the temple (2 Sam. 7:12-15), but it isn't recorded that He announced the name of the son at that time. Amnon and Absalom had already been born, and the announcement sounds as if the designated son would be

born in the future. First Chronicles 22:6-10 indicates that at some point the Lord had told David that Solomon would be his successor (see 28:6-10; 29:1). Whether they knew it or not, both Amnon and Absalom were fighting a losing battle.

7. It seems strange that Jonadab would make this announcement, because by doing so, he was almost confessing that he knew something about the plot. However, David and his servants knew that Jonadab was Amnon's confidant, and no doubt they concluded that he and Amnon had discussed Absalom's attitude and concluded that there was danger in the air. Jonadab was too shrewd a man to implicate himself before the king.

8. See "Of Revenge" in *The Essays of Francis Bacon*.

9. God solved this problem for lost sinners by sending His Son to die on the cross, and thus He upheld the law but at the same time provided salvation for all who trust Christ. See Romans 3:19-31.

10. How heavy was the hair that Absalom's barber cut from his head? It all depends on the weight of the "royal shekel" (v. 26). If it was 11.5 grams, then the haircut produced about five pounds of hair. Baldness was ridiculed in Israel (2 Kings 2:23).

11. The parallels between Absalom and Samson are interesting. Both were distinguished by their hair, for Samson was a Nazirite (Jud. 13:1-5), and both set fields on fire (Jud. 15:4-5). The loss of his hair caused Samson's defeat (Jud. 16:17ff), and it's probable that Absalom's thick hair helped to trap his head in the tree branches, where Joab found him and killed him (2 Sam. 18:9-17).

Chapter 7

1. The word "demagogue" comes from two Greek words: *demos* (people) and *agogos* (guiding). A true leader uses his authority to help people, but a demagogue uses people to gain authority. Demagogues pretend to be concerned about the needs of the people, but their only concern is to get into power and enjoy the fruits of their dishonesty.

2. Hebrew texts vary from "four" to "forty." If forty is the correct number, we don't know the starting point—forty years from what event? Some chronologists date Absalom's rebellion at between 1023 and 1027 BC. This would be approximately forty years from David's

anointing by Samuel, but why select that event? It seems reasonable to accept "four" as the correct number and date it from Amnon's reconciliation with his father (14:33).

3. Most students identify Psalms 3, 4, 41, 55, 61–63, and 143 as "exile psalms," and some add Psalms 25, 28, 58, and 109. Both Psalms 41 and 55 indicate that David was not well, and see 61:6-7. If indeed David was ill, then he was unable to meet the people and hear their problems; and Absalom took advantage of this situation.

4. David once lied about attending a feast as a device to deceive King Saul (1 Sam. 20:6). Thus do our sins find us out.

5. David faced a similar test when he was serving as commander of the bodyguard of Achish, king of the Philistines (1 Sam. 29).

6. David's statement "Behold, here am I" reminds us of Abraham (Gen. 22:1, 11), Jacob (Gen. 31:11; 46:2), Moses (Ex. 3:4), Samuel (1 Sam. 3:4, 16) and Isaiah (Isa. 6:8). It is a statement of surrender.

7. *God Tells the Man Who Cares* (Christian Publications, 1970), p. 9.

8. It was at Bahurim that David's wife Michal said good-bye to her second husband as she was returned to David, and the man wept bitterly (3:13-16). Now it was David who was weeping.

Chapter 8

1. In 279 BC, the army of Pyrrhus, king of Epirus, defeated the Romans at Asculum at such great cost that he said, "One more such victory and we are lost."

2. For a detailed study of the speeches of Ahithophel and Hushai, and why God used Hushai's counsel, see chapters 1–4 of my book *Preaching and Teaching with Imagination* (Baker Books).

3. The word in 18:14 translated "darts" in the KJV and "javelins" in the NIV can mean rod, staff, or even scepter. They were probably javelins sharpened at one end. Joab thrust them into Absalom's body, and then the ten men around the tree finished the job.

4. The scene reminds us of Eli the priest waiting at the gate for news concerning the ark of the covenant (1 Sam. 4:12ff).

5. This is the familiar Hebrew word *shalom*, which among other things means "peace, health, well-being." David's uses the word in his questions: "Is the young man Absalom *shalom*?" (vv. 29, 32).

6. *The Metropolitan Tabernacle Pulpit*, vol. 24, p. 505.

Chapter 9

1. "The people" in 2 Samuel is a phrase that identifies David's followers, especially his army. See 15:17, 23-24, 30; 16:14; 17:2-3, 16, 22; 18:1-4, 6, 16; 19:2-3, 8-9, 39. Another term for his army is "the servants of David" (2:13, 15, 17, 30-31; 3:22; 8:2, 6, 14; 10:2, 4; 11:9, 11, 13, 17; 12:18; 15:15; 16:6; 18:7, 9; 19:6; 20:6).

2. Shimei identified himself with "the house of Joseph" (v. 20), and this is the first time this phrase is used in the Old Testament. It refers to the ten tribes headed by Ephraim, Joseph's younger son. The ten northern tribes were often called "Ephraim" or "sons of Joseph."

3. The KJV translation "to Jerusalem" in verse 25 should read, "from Jerusalem."

4. The "Absalom episode" began with David kissing Absalom after his son's two years of house arrest (14:33), and ended with David kissing Barzillai.

5. *Henry IV, Part 2*, act 3, scene 1.

Chapter 10

1. Joab killed Abner because Abner had killed Joab's brother Asahel, and it was done near Gibeon, where Joab met Amasa (2:12ff). Perhaps the memory of his brother's murder aroused Joab, even though Amasa had nothing to do with it.

2. Why the Gibeonites didn't bring the matter before David much earlier is a mystery, for as resident aliens in the land, they had their civil rights. During the first part of his reign, David was securing and extending the kingdom, and in the last years he was dealing with the troubles caused by his own sins, so perhaps it took time to get the king's ear. By sending drought and famine, the Lord kept the terms of the covenant (Lev. 26:18-20; Deut. 28:23-24).

3. The Law of Moses gave resident aliens certain rights, and Israel was warned not to oppress the strangers in the land (Ex. 22:21; Lev. 19:34; Deut. 24:17). Apparently neither Joshua's vow nor the Law of Moses restrained Saul from trying to liquidate the Gibeonites.

4. But David also made a similar promise to Saul (1 Sam. 24:20-22),

and here he was having Saul's descendants slain. However, the killing of five men wasn't the equivalent of wiping out all of a man's family.

5. We're told in 6:23 that Michal died without having any children, so the text should read Merab (see NIV). She was Saul's daughter by Ahinoam (1 Sam. 14:49) and was married to Adriel (1 Sam. 18:17-19).

6. The Hebrew text reads "descendants of Rapha." The word means "giant" (Deut. 2:11, 20; Josh. 12:4; 13:12; 17:15; 1 Chron. 20:4, 6, 8.)

Chapter 11

1. In Ezekiel 1, the prophet saw God's glorious throne on a magnificent crystal platform, with cherubim at each corner, like "wheels" carrying the throne from place to place. The image of God's throne like a chariot reminds us that He can come down from heaven to help His people and nothing can thwart Him.

2. Light as an image of God is frequently found in Scripture (Ps. 84:11; Isa. 60:19-20; Ezek. 1:4, 27; Dan. 2:22; Micah 7:8; Mal. 4:2; Luke 2:32; John 8:12; 1 Tim. 6:16; 1 John 1:5; Rev. 21:23.)

Chapter 12

1. In the Old Testament, God viewed the rulers of Israel as shepherds, which explains passages like Jeremiah 10:21, 12:10, 23:1-8, 25:36; Ezekiel 34:1-18; Zechariah 10:2, 11:15-17. The word "pastor" means "shepherd."

2. Second Samuel 8:13 gives David credit for the great victory against the Edomites, while 1 Chronicles 18:12 attributes the victory to Abishai. The inscription of Palm. 60 states that Joab was also a part of the event. It's likely that David was in charge and Joab and his brother Abishai commanded the field forces. It was customary in those days for the king to get the credit for such victories (see 2 Sam. 12:26-31).

3. For an excellent comparative chart of David's mighty men, see pages 478-479 of the Old Testament volume of *The Bible Knowledge Commentary*, edited by John Walvoord and Roy Zuck (Victor).

4. Some students think that the three who brought the water from the Bethlehem well were the men named in verses 8-12, but verse 13 seems to indicate they were a different trio, a part of "The Thirty."

5. The two terms "The Three" and "The Thirty" are found frequently in this chapter. For "The Three" see verses 9, 13, 16-19, 22, 23; for "The Thirty" see verses 13, 23-24. In 1 Chronicles 11, "The Three" are mentioned in verses 12, 15, 18-21, 24, 25; and "The Thirty" in verses 15, 25, and 42.

6. For a study of these four appearances of Satan and how they apply to believers today, see my book *The Strategy of Satan* (Tyndale House).

7. First Chronicles 21:5 records 1,100,000 men, but we need to remember that Joab didn't complete the census (1 Chron. 27:23-24) and different sums were recorded at different times during the nine months of the survey. Also, note that 2 Samuel 24:9 specifies "800,000 valiant men," that is, an experienced standing army, while there could have been another 300,000 men who were of age but not seasoned in battle. This gives us the 1,100,000 total of 1 Chronicles 21:5.

8. The prophet Gad first appears in Scripture after David fled from Saul (1 Sam. 22:5). He must have been an expert on Jewish liturgy because he assisted David in organizing the Levites for their part in the temple worship services. He also kept an official record of the events of David's reign (1 Chron. 29:29).

9. More than once God sent plagues to Israel to chasten His people (Num. 11:31-34; 14:36-38; 16:46-50; 21:4-9; 26:9-10). Of course, this was in agreement with His covenant, which the people had broken.

Chapter 13

1. It's too bad that many well-meaning preachers misinterpret 1 Corinthians 3:9-23 and preach about "building your life." You can make that application, but the basic interpretation has to do with building the local church. For an exposition of this passage, see my book *Be Wise* (Victor).

2. The psalm certainly fits David's experiences described in 1 Samuel 24 and 1 Chronicles 21. His pride led him to sin (vv. 6-7) and the nation was under the penalty of death. But God answered his plea for deliverance, and His anger lasted for a short time.

3. Adoram wasn't a popular man. After Solomon's death, Solomon's son Rehoboam took the throne. The people were tired of Solomon's

taxes and vast building programs, and they stoned Adoram to death (2 Kings 11:18).

4. First Chronicles 26:18 in the KJV has been a popular verse with people who like to criticize the Scriptures: "At Parbar westward, four at the causeway, and two at Parbar." What does "Parbar" mean? Many Hebrew scholars say it means "colonnade" and refers to an area west of the temple proper. The NLT reads, "Six were assigned each day to the west gate, four to the gateway leading up to the Temple, and two to the courtyard." A footnote says that "courtyard" could also be translated "colonnade," but "the meaning of the Hebrew is uncertain."

5. Forgive a personal note at this point. Back in the Fifties, when I was pastoring my first church, the Lord led us into a building program. I'm not a builder and I have a problem even reading a blueprint, and I was very worried. One day in my personal devotional time, during the course of my regular Bible reading, I came to 1 Chronicles 28:20, and the Lord gave it to me as His promise of success. It carried me through.

Chapter One

David, King of Judah
(2 Sam. 1:1–2:7; 1 Chron. 10:1-10)

1. With what events does 2 Samuel begin and end?

2. One of the major themes of 2 Samuel is restoration. What was restored?

3. How did God work in David's life when he was in exile and pursued by Saul?

4. How did David and his camp respond to the death of Saul? Why did this surprise the Amalekites?

5. What were the qualities or achievements of Saul that David highlighted in his lament?

6. For what purposes might David have composed and taught the funeral song?

7. When making decisions, David sought the Lord's will. Why might a believer neglect to seek the Lord's will in decision making? Why is it essential?

8. Why was Hebron important in Jewish history?

9. What similarities can be seen between the life of David and that of Jesus Christ?

10. In what way do people today "put human leaders ahead of God's anointed king" (Jesus)? What problems does this create?

Chapter Two

David Watches and Waits
(2 Sam. 2:8-4:12)

1. What does it mean that David "learned to build with the materials at hand"? In what circumstance in your life would it be helpful for you to take that perspective?

2. Who was Abner? Why did he reject David's kingship?

3. How do we see the story of David, Abner, and Ish-bosheth duplicated in politics and religion of our day?

4. How did God view David's multiple wives? What were some consequences of David having so many family members?

5. Why did David and Abner use "shuttle diplomacy"?

6. How did the return of Michal to David help resolve the situation?

7. When Joab reproached David after Abner was received peacefully, how did David respond? What did this mean?

8. What could David have done better with his family? How can a person know when to be "weak" (restrained and gentle) and when to be tough?

9. Sin and death seemed to reign during these early years of David's kingship. In what ways did God's grace also reign?

10. What must God's people do to "reign in life by Jesus Christ"?

Chapter Three

David, King of Israel

(2 Sam. 5-6; 1 Chron. 3:4-8;
11:1-9; 13:5-16:3)

1. In what condition was the nation of Israel when David became king? What did God, through David, make Israel into?

2. What was the foundation of the Jewish nation?

3. Why was Jerusalem an ideal choice for a new capital city?

4. Why was it necessary for David to seek the Lord's will for the second battle with the Philistines? From where might David have learned this tip?

5. Why was it so important to David that the ark of the covenant be in Jerusalem?

6. What mistakes were made in the moving of the ark of the covenant? What is a possible reason God's judgment was so swift and fierce toward Uzzah?

7. What lesson can the church learn from this today? ("No amount of _____ or _____ can compensate for _____.")

8. What characterized David's dancing before the Lord? Why did the church fathers eventually ban dancing in the church?

9. Michal criticized David's worship of the Lord. When has your enthusiasm for the Lord been criticized?

10. How did the death of Jonathan and the barrenness of Michal contribute to God's unfolding plan?

Chapter Four

David's Dynasty, Kindness, and Conquests
(2 Sam. 7-10; 1 Chron. 17-19)

1. In 2 Samuel 7-10, in what four activities was David involved?

2. When David's kingdom was at peace, what did he want to do?

3. What were the main points of the message God gave Nathan for David?

4. What did God want David to focus on instead of building?

5. What are five different aspects of the "rest" God promised to His people?

6. In what ways was David's response to God's covenant with him a good example for us to follow? What covenant has God made with believers?

7. What great works did Israel have to perform on earth? To what great work has God called all Christians today?

8. What are the two themes in 2 Samuel 9? How do we see both themes in David's treatment of Mephibosheth? How does Jesus show both kindness and kingship?

9. How does David's treatment of Mephibosheth illustrate a believer's spiritual experience on earth?

10. What major mistake did Hanun make? How can you avoid making this same mistake? (See Psalm 1:1-2.)

Chapter Five

David's Disobedience, Deception, and Discipline
(2 Sam. 11-12)

1. What did Spurgeon mean by saying, "God does not allow his children to sin successfully"?

2. What principles for our free time can we learn from David's mistakes?

3. What should David have done when he first glimpsed Bathsheba?

4. Once David heard Bathsheba had conceived his child, how did he try to cover up?

5. When have you scrambled to cover up a sin? What should a believer do when caught in sin?

6. Why was Nathan's story of the ewe lamb so effective in making its intended point?

7. What were the consequences of David's sins of lust, deceit, and murder? How did David find forgiveness of those sins?

8. What is chastening? When have you recognized chastening in your life?

9. What answers are available for those who struggle with the question, "Why does God permit evil in the world?"

10. What did the birth of Solomon signify to David and Bathsheba? After falling into sin, how can a person start anew?

Chapter Six

David's Unruly Sons
(2 Sam. 13–14)

1. How did David respond as he faced the problems brought on by his children?

2. When a person like Amnon feels attraction to someone who is off-limits (as Amnon experienced), what should he or she do about it? What did Amnon do?

3. In what way might David's bad example have influenced Amnon?

4. How did this rape ruin Tamar's life?

5. Why didn't David or Absalom immediately confront or punish Amnon?

6. What part of David's bad example might have influenced Absalom in his act of revenge?

7. Why is revenge never the solution? In what ways is Jesus the perfect example for us regarding revenge?

8. How did David compromise between Absalom's exile and full reconciliation? How did Absalom feel about this arrangement?

9. David's decision about Absalom was complex. What would you have done? Why? When dealing with a complex situation, what should you be sure to do?

10. In what ways were David and Absalom reconciled? What was left unsaid or unresolved?

Chapter Seven

David's Escape to the Wilderness
(2 Sam. 15:1-16:14)

1. During David's escape to the wilderness, how did he see God's hand at work?

2. Why were David's faith and submission to the Lord heightened at this dark time?

3. How did David, in earlier days, win the hearts of the people? How was Absalom's way different?

4. What unexpected consequences of David's sin with Bathsheba surfaced later with Ahithophel?

5. Why was Hebron chosen by Absalom for the site of his insurrection?

6. What strong conviction about the Lord did David have throughout his perilous circumstances? How can that encourage us today in our own difficulties?

7. When David was suffering the pain of betrayal by someone close to him, what good model did he leave for us to follow?

8. What mistake did David make with Ziba? Why was David vulnerable to that mistake?

9. Why did David allow Shimei's abuse to continue?

10. What similarities are there between the life of Christ and the life of David?

Chapter Eight

David's Bittersweet Victory
(2 Sam. 16:15–18:33)

1. Why was David willing to flee and allow a bloodless takeover of the kingdom?

2. When making decisions, what did Absalom substitute for seeking the Lord? When have you caught yourself doing the same thing? Why do we sometimes fall into this situation?

3. Why did Absalom take his father's concubines?

4. What different approach did the Lord direct Hushai to take when giving counsel to Absalom? Why was it successful?

5. How did God use the wife in Bahurim? What does this teach us about spontaneous acts of service?

6. What can we learn from the way Ahithophel's life came to a close?

7. How did David continue to show mercy to Absalom even in battle? What did Absalom deserve?

8. What do we deserve from God? What do we get through faith in Christ?

9. How did Absalom's life end? What did hanging on a tree signify to an Israelite?

10. How is the heart of God revealed in the heart of David as he wept over Absalom?

Chapter Nine

David's Return and Renewed Problems
(2 Sam. 19:1-40)

1. What five steps did David take for the healing of the nation of Israel?

2. What did David temporarily set aside while he was grieving over Absalom? How can leaders still lead while suffering?

3. What did David neglect to do during his troubles with Absalom?

4. Why did David first choose the tribe of Judah to help him unify the people?

5. What positive result came from David's granting amnesty to the rebel army?

6. How did David deal with Shimei? Why?

7. Why did David appoint Amasa to be his commander instead of Joab?

8. What complicated situation did David face when Mephibosheth met with him? What was Mephibosheth's goal in that meeting?

9. How did David reward Barzillai for his kindness? How did Barzillai respond?

10. How do you reward people for their kindness to you?

Chapter Ten

David's New Struggles
(2 Sam. 19:41–21:22;
1 Chron. 20:4-8

1. What four conflicts did David still need to deal with after Absalom's death?

2. A crisis can bring out the best or worst in people. What does a crisis bring out in you? What makes the difference?

3. What did Sheba say that lit "the fires of conflict"?

4. How did the woman of Abel act wisely to save the city?

5. What led to the meeting of Amasa with Joab and Abishai? Why did Joab kill Amasa?

6. What did Saul do to bring down the delayed judgment of a three-year drought during David's reign?

7. What legal retribution did the Gibeonites ask for the sins of Saul?

8. How did the Lord respond after the seven men were killed?

9. How did Rizpah, in her grief, show love and courage?

10. What truth can we glean from this harsh judgment?

Chapter Eleven

David's Song of Victory
(2 Sam. 22; Ps. 18)

1. In David's song of victory, what was David giving thanks for?

2. How did David describe the Lord in his song of praise?

3. What does the image of God as a rock mean to you?

4. How can you follow David's example when facing opposition?

5. How did God build David into a leader? When have you noticed God using hard times to mold you?

6. How was David able to live a blameless life while Saul was pursuing and threatening him? Since every person is a sinner, in what way was David blameless?

7. What is essential to "knowing and doing the will of God and pleasing His heart"? How can we achieve this goal?

8. In what way did David's body belong to the Lord?

9. What do we need to remember as we read of David's vicious victories over other people?

10. When did God reveal His plan to include Gentiles in salvation? How were David and the nation of Israel part of this grand, sovereign plan?

Chapter Twelve

David's Memories and Mistakes
(2 Sam. 23-24;
1 Chron. 11:10-41; 21:1-26)

1. What three portraits of David are seen in 2 Samuel 23–24?

2. What are some of the ways God used David, a "nobody"?

3. When deciding to follow a leader, what should you look for? What happens if those qualities are missing?

4. We might compare ourselves unfavorably to "mighty men," but how does God measure our worth?

5. Why did the three men risk their lives to get David a cup of water? How did David respond when they returned?

6. "Doing small things because we love Christ turns them into great things." What small things have you done lately because you love Christ?

7. Why was it wrong for David to take a census?

8. Why did God give David a choice of judgments? What did David choose? Why?

9. In the midst of the plague, what message did the prophet Gad bring?

10. What were David's two greatest sins? How did God bring good from them? How can this fact bring comfort to us?

Chapter Thirteen

David's Legacy
(1 Chron. 22-29)

1. How is David's life and faith still enriching the church today?

2. What parallels can be drawn between the building of the temple and the building of the church?

3. In what ways did David encourage his son Solomon concerning the building of the temple?

4. What aspect of the church was foreshadowed by the variety of people fulfilling duties in the temple?

5. What was more important than the organization of the workers and the building project?

6. How did David challenge the workers? Of what did David remind them?

7. What four gifts did David give Solomon?

8. What gifts will you give or leave behind for your children and your church?

9. What can we learn about God and life from David's prayer in 2 Samuel 29:10-21?

10. How would you summarize David's legacy?